SHOWING UP:

A Comprehensive Guide to Comfort and Connection

New Degree Press

Copyright © 2022 Jen Marr
All rights reserved.

First Published 2019

No part of this publication may be reproduced or distributed in any form or by any means, electronic or mechanical, or stored in a database or retrieval system, without prior written permission.

Contact Information
inspiringcomfort.com (http://inspiringcomfort.com/)
info@inspiringcomfort.com

ISBN   978-8-88504-900-9   *Paperback*

Printed in USA

"People don't care what you know, until they know that you care."

—John Maxwell

To my amazing tribe: My loving husband Dave, and beautiful daughters, Erika, Ashlyn & Audrey.

For your incredible "Marrway" love, support and understanding of this work.

For each missed minute of being together because of it and for knowing when to comfort me when I need it. You've always showed up for me. In good times and bad. You have my heart. Always and forever.

CONTENTS

8   Foreword by Dr. John Draper
12   How It All Began

PART 1: THE CASE FOR COMFORT

22   The Empathy & Compassion Action Gap
26   The Definition
32   A Timeline of Care
36   Where We Are Today
42   The Dangers of Isolation
46   The New Leadership Skill

PART 2: THE PROCESS

54   The Awkward Zone
62   The Process & The Science
74   The Mindset & The Choice
80   Who All Needs Care

PART 3: SHOWING UP

92   Changing Our Perspective
96   Cycle of Support
98   The Full Body of Comfort
102   Heart, Ears, Eyes, Hands, Feet, & Soul All Play a Part
160   Applying the Skill

PART 4: CREATING A CULTURE OF CARE

164   What is a Culture of Care?
169   What Experts Are Saying
173   The Cost of Not Caring

PART 5: WHO SHOWS UP BEST?

178   The Magic of a Dog

WE ALL HAVE A ROLE TO PLAY
HOW COMFORT SAVES LIVES

By Dr. John Draper, Executive Director of National Suicide Prevention Lifeline (988) and Executive VP of National Networks, Vibrant Emotional Health

I first met Jen Marr at the New York State Suicide Prevention Conference in 2017. She was bringing care and support to crisis response work through animal therapy utilizing golden retrievers. We spoke about how much better the world would be if we could care for each other the way our pets cared for us. I have watched her essential work in *human* care grow over these past five years.

Jen is fond of saying what loneliness is. It's not being alone, but it's feeling alone, as if no one really cares about you. That's often what leads people to suicidal despair—having to go through whatever they're having to go through feeling like other people just don't care or that they are a burden to them. Perhaps if somebody was with them to help them deal with it, they might be able to feel less overwhelmed and more capable.

As a psychology student, I was instructed in the basic essentials of what constitutes a truly therapeutic relationship, as postulated by the father of Humanistic Psychology, Dr. Carl Rogers. Rogers' three fundamental relationship elements include unconditional positive regard, genuineness, and empathy. If I feel that someone cares for me without judgment (unconditional positive regard), who is authentic and honest in his/her reactions to what I say and feel (genuineness), and who seems to understand and appreciate how I feel (empathy), I will feel safe to be and feel free to strive toward becoming my best self. Research has been clear that the most powerful influence over whether therapy is effective or not is the quality of the therapeutic relationship. Decades of studies continuously point to these three Rogerian principles as the building blocks of an effective therapeutic relationship. In my work to develop national standards for crisis counselors on hotlines, we have also found that these relationship factors are the most important ones in assisting people in suicidal distress.

We know, and the research shows, that when somebody is helping you deal with an extremely overwhelming task, it feels less overwhelming and essentially becomes something you can cope through. But feeling like you're alone and believing you're alone because no one else cares can often lead a person to spiral into despair.

Comfort is an essential component in overcoming this despair and creating meaningful connections for all of us. Jen's passion for this work has been driven by her belief that comfort is critical to promoting more connectedness in our world, and this evidence-based skill can be taught in a simple way. As a result, she has researched human care and interviewed experts toward writing the book you now have in your hands: *Showing Up: A Comprehensive Guide to Comfort and Connection.*

It's crucial to learn these skills when we are attuned to a fast-paced world where mobile technologies, the unprecedented 24/7/365 prevalence of media and information, competitive performance pressures, and divisive ideologies dominate our everyday experience. In our first twenty years of this century, we also see escalating anxiety, depression, and suicide rates, especially

> In this book, you will learn how to overcome awkwardness and uncover how to provide care and support in ways that are simple to those around you.

among our younger populations. Could teaching comfort in our homes, schools, and communities help us overcome our looming cultural "connection deficit disorder"?

Whatever we can do to reach out and help each other and be there—not just on our phones but in our lives—will matter. People who are close to us can say certain things that we can't say on the hotlines and that they can't say in therapy offices. Things such as "I love you," and "You mean so much to me," and "I need you. I need you in my life." You just won't hear those things elsewhere. But those things help people feel cared about and cared for. And those kinds of things are the lifeblood that keep people living and smiling, getting them through not only today but tomorrow.

Perhaps now is the time to develop these critical life skills. In this book, you will learn how to overcome awkwardness and uncover how to provide care and support in ways that are simple to those around you.

The mental health community can't do it alone. The world needs all of us to know how to connect with those who are struggling too.

> Whatever we can do to reach out and help each other be there— not just on our phones but in our lives—will matter.

About Dr. John Draper: Dr. Draper has more than thirty years of experience in crisis intervention and suicide prevention work and is considered one of the nation's leading experts in crisis contact center practices (hotline, online chat, SMS services, etc.). He oversees all aspects of the federally funded National Suicide Prevention Lifeline network (988), which consists of over 190 member crisis centers across the country. Dr. Draper frequently presents at national conferences on subjects related to best practices in crisis intervention and suicide prevention as well as the use of innovative technologies (text, chat, other online programs, etc.) in helping persons in emotional distress. Dr. Draper also frequently discusses the role of persons with lived experience of suicide (attempt survivors, loss survivors, etc.) in suicide prevention. Dr. Draper has been interviewed and quoted in a wide variety of print and broadcast media, including CNN, The New York Times, The Washington Post, ABC News, USA Today, CBS Sunday Morning, and TIME among others.

"I find it shelter to speak to you."

—*Emily Dickinson*

LEARNING COMFORT: HOW IT ALL BEGAN

How the trails in my life came together to open my eyes to a growing need for comfort and equipped me to move forward with this work.

Have you ever wondered where the breadcrumbs of your life are leading? I know I have. I've always questioned why I'm walking this earth at this place and time in history.

So, it hit me one day that my entire life has left behind tons of little breadcrumbs that offer clues, laying out what I'm meant to do in life. I believe this with my whole heart.

The combination of all of these breadcrumbs has put me on the trail to discover the significance of comfort in our world.

So, let's consider that we have three trails we walk down:
1. Our **"Brain Trail"**—What we are good at and what we do—Our minds at work
2. Our **"Heart Trail"**—Where our hearts lead us and what we love—Our hearts at work
3. Our **"Circumstances Trail"**—What happens to us in life—Circumstances and experiences at work

These three trails combine to lead to our life's work. For me, my life's work braids entrepreneurship, tragedy, and a desire to help.

My "Brain Trail" travels down to entrepreneurship. Every job I've ever done has started with a blank piece of paper. I love to develop projects: envision them, start them, and grow them. Sometimes I've gotten paid, sometimes I didn't, and sometimes I lost money trying something that didn't work. For me, it was always about creating something, making something better, or doing something different.

My "Circumstances Trail" has repeatedly traveled through crisis and tragedy zones. My nickname growing up was Di-

saster Annie. I almost drowned twice, had the Heimlich done on me as I choked on beef stroganoff, and was on a first-name basis in the ER. If there was a crisis or disaster, I was sure to be nearby. This pattern followed me into adulthood as I found myself living through terrorist attacks in London and Boston, a major flood in Minnesota, 9/11 with my husband in New York City, a tornado in Wisconsin, and the 1989 earthquake in San Francisco.

> We are surrounded by sadness, sorrow, and a culture that must relearn the skills to support and comfort each other.

My "Heart Trail" grew as Disaster Annie dealt with each new crisis. As each horrible event happened to me and to those around me, I felt an increasing desire to help. My eyes were opened to everyday pain in those who were suffering. I was led to help. It burned in my heart to help. And with each new tragedy, I felt more equipped to help.

These three trails came together in the aftermath of the tragedy at Sandy Hook Elementary and the bombing at the Boston Marathon.

These two back-to-back events caused both my brain and my heart to search for answers and led me to take a deep dive into how we care for each other. They led me to spend years responding to suicides, drug overdoses, car accidents, cancer, tragedy, illness, and sadness.

SEARCHING FOR A SOLUTION

I remember the day I knew we needed to do more like it was yesterday.

During a crisis response to a high school, I found myself sitting in a circle with the best friends of the brother of a student who died. They were talking about their friend and feeling helpless. One by one, those students sitting in the circle all admitted the same thing.

Not one of them had reached out to their friend yet. Not one.

And it wasn't because they didn't care. I saw the empathy and compassion these students felt for their friend. They just didn't know what to do with those emotions. Their phones were in their hands, but they didn't know what to say, so they ended up saying nothing. Their poor friend, grieving at home, was left wondering why no one cared to reach out.

The one struggling the most was left to struggle even more because no one was reaching out to check on him.

These students experienced the Awkward Zone™. They were used to happy Instagrams and funny snaps, sporting events, concerts, and talk of college. No one prepared them for being the broken one or supporting the broken one.

I found myself wondering each time I left a thirty-six or seventy-two-hour crisis response: "What happens to these shattered lives now?"

In my head, again and again, was this phrase—encouraging me to take it on: "You can give someone comfort, and they will be comforted for a day. If you teach someone how to comfort, they will feel comfort for a lifetime."

Could it work?

That phrase led me to form Inspiring Comfort LLC, write this book and take on this mission. I felt in the depths of my soul that we had to do more.

> You can give someone comfort, and they will be comforted for a day. If you teach someone how to comfort, they will feel comfort for a lifetime.

WHAT I'M LEARNING ABOUT THE POWER OF COMFORT

Comfort focuses on someone else and intentionally acts to bring them some hope, bringing us hope at the same time.

Comfort doesn't take away the pain. It gives us the ability to handle it with a friend who cares.

Comfort is the most powerful form of connection that exists.

Comfort puts empathy and compassion into action, going much deeper than random kindness.

We acknowledge the importance of emotions when we comfort each other.

We find true comfort in people, not material things.

We have become experts in maintaining a grand scope of friendships and amateurs in genuine intimacy and care. Unwittingly, we have sacrificed everything on the altar of self-sufficiency—only to discover that we have sold our souls to isolation."

– *Sandy Oshiro Rosen*

PART ONE

THE CASE FOR COMFORT

The Empathy & Compassion Action Gap

The Definition

A Timeline of Care

Where We Are Today

Dangers of Isolation

The New Leadership Skill

EMPATHY, SYMPATHY, COMPASSION, AND THE ACTION GAP

I never set out to do this work. This work found me after years of observing how those hurting hurt even more when people around them don't know how to adequately support them. After almost ten years of being a practitioner of care—giving, learning, researching, feeling, needing, and teaching how to care for others—I want to share what I am learning.

EMPATHY, SYMPATHY, AND COMPASSION

Needing to feel cared for and feeling the need to care for others are at the core of our humanity.

Empathy, sympathy, and compassion are at the foundation of these needs. However, empathy, sympathy, and compassion are emotions, and emotions can also get in our way when it comes to actually putting these needs into action.

The dictionary lists empathy, sympathy, and compassion as nouns, not verbs—things, not actions—and so acting on that "thing" can get tricky. Feelings of awkwardness can take over and paralyze us. Feelings of fear can cause us to doubt what to do when we don't have the skills and tools to know how to do it.

How can you best learn to act on your emotions (your nouns) in a way that brings appropriate support to those hurting? With verbs, of course! In the case of acting on empathy, sympathy, and compassion, comfort is the strongest, most resilient community-building verb out there (more on that in the next section).

Think of it this way. In the last section, I spoke about the needs of those struggling with tragic life events. They need to be seen, heard, validated, loved, understood, comforted. To be cared for is to have actions applied to you. It's impossible to be "empathied" or "compassioned" by someone else. These aren't even words because nouns don't act.

I started on this journey of comfort because I was observing that it wasn't enough to feel these critical emotions. What people did with these feelings mattered.

THE DREADED APATHY

What about those who don't even feel caring emotions? Those who are crushed and broken from years of abuse, neglect, or some other awful circumstance only indifference. They only feel indifference. What about them?

It's crucial for their overall well-being to feel the emotions of empathy, sympathy, and compassion. They desperately need to feel cared for and to feel the need to care for others. For this to happen, actions are required for those dormant emotions to awaken so they can be cultivated. Once again, comforting actions may be the best way for this to occur.

DATA REFLECTS THE EMOTION VERSUS ACTION GAP

Part of what our comfort programming does when teaching this skill is survey and assess all those who participate. Tens of thousands of data points later, these simple facts stand out and confirm what I saw in the field.

Roughly **80%** FEEL THEY CAN SEE THOSE WHO ARE IN PAIN.	Roughly **80%** FEEL THEY ARE NEVER, RARELY, OR ONLY SOMETIMES SEEN IN THEIR OWN STRUGGLES.	Roughly **75%** DO NOT FEEL EQUIPPED TO KNOW WHAT TO SAY AND DO FOR THOSE STRUGGLING.

Ponder these three points for a minute. This data holds true for all age groups, all demographics, and all training types.

What does it mean when everyone says, "I can see *you* when you struggle, but no one sees *me* when I struggle?" It means we have a massive emotion versus action gap, and this gap must be tackled.

Why is this happening? It's right there. People don't know what to say and do. They feel an emotion but don't know how to apply it, so they avoid action.

Let's tackle this.

COMFORT:
THE VERB

*When someone is hopeless,
it takes another person to bring hope.*

Let's talk about the word "comfort." It sounds soft and fuzzy — I get it. So why am I so passionate about this word? It begins with the word itself. Let's look at the Latin origins of the word comfort:

COM: "together with" — it's the core of the word community.

FORT: "strength" — a fort is a strong, protective barrier.

But this strong, actionable, resilient verb has been overshadowed in our current world by its cozy, inactive noun cousin.

VERB vs NOUN

Consider these two forms of the word comfort with this skimmed down definition from the Merriam Webster Dictionary: a verb vs. a noun and an action vs. a feeling.

com · fort | \ ˈkəm(p)-fərt \
comforted; comforting; comforts

verb

Definition of comfort (Entry 1 of 2)

transitive verb
1 : to give strength and hope to
2 : to ease the grief or trouble of

noun

Definition of comfort (Entry 2 of 2)

1 **a**   : a feeling of relief or encouragement
    b   : contented well-being
2   : a satisfying or enjoyable experience

*The verb of comfort takes courageous action and brings strength & hope, while the noun of comfort only **feels** comfortable.*

STRENGTH & HOPE

It's in helping others where the real beauty of life can be found.

In our programs, we frequently ask participants what comfort means to them. The result is this heart, scaled by the number of times each word was mentioned. The heart of comfort: what being comforted means.

When emotions are cultivated through actions of care, this is the result:

Just imagine if you were the reason someone felt all of these things. Imagine how it would make you feel in return. This is the beauty of caring for each other. It doesn't have to be hard. Let's break it down.

LOOKING BACK TO MOVE FORWARD: THE EVOLUTION OF COMFORT

No matter how long you have traveled in the wrong direction, you always have the choice to turn around.
–Heather K. Jones

I grew up in rural Wisconsin in the sixties and seventies and am only a few generations away from my brave ancestors who escaped poverty by immigrating to America. One set of grandparents farmed land given in the Homestead Act in Helenville, Wisconsin; the other set ran a "filling station" in Readlyn, Iowa. As a result, my parents were raised with very little financially, but they grew up rich in love and knew what it meant to need each other. I'll readily admit that my parents were the best teachers of care a person could ask for, and this became the foundation of my childhood—a home that had more love than money and was filled with time with cousins and aunts and uncles and grandparents. A true tribe.

Part of this childhood was frequently helping my parents help those who were dealing with tragedy, crisis, or loss. I don't recall there being an awkwardness. We had no choice. We just went and most times hung out at the house doing whatever needed to be done. As a child without a phone in hand, I had to find a way to occupy myself: washing dishes, taking out the trash, or any other odd job I could find.

When I was about ten, an acquaintance of my parents' was tragically killed. I didn't really know this family, but over time I became very familiar with each of them and their friends. I would listen to my parents' phone calls with Ellen, the surviving widow, as she took over the family business and navigated life. Ellen's daughter Linda taught me how to play the oboe, and each year I got to know them better and better.

Still today, Ellen is a dear friend I stay in touch with. I would have never known this family the way I do today if I hadn't been at my parents' side as they cared for the family over the years.

But I also remember the broader community that kicked in. We were not at all the only family helping out; it was a community effort. Usually organized through the church where everyone saw each other every week, I was taught to give hugs, send cards, and show love and compassion for all of those who were hurting. It's just what we did: things like remembering anniversaries and birthdays of those who had passed, and bringing over fruit baskets during the holidays, knowing they would be going through a rough time.

What has changed since then?

> "It wasn't all that long ago that it was standard in our culture for people to officially be in mourning for a full year. They wore black. They didn't go to parties. They didn't smile a whole lot. And everybody accepted their period of mourning; no one ridiculed a mother in black or asked her stupid questions about why she was still so sad. Obviously, this is no longer accepted practice; mourners are encouraged to quickly move on, turn the corner, get back to work, think of the positive, be grateful for what is left, have another baby, and other unkind, unfeeling, obtuse, and downright cruel comments. What does this say about us—other than we're terribly uncomfortable with death, with grief, with mourning, with loss—or we're so self-absorbed that we easily forget the profound suffering the loss of a child created in the shattered parents and remaining children."
>
> —KAY WARREN, FACEBOOK POST

CREATING A TIMELINE OF HOW WE SHOW CARE

Human behaviors of care were relatively unchanged from the beginning of recorded history until well into the 1900s. Each area where we have historically cared for, supported, and comforted each other has been flipped on its head in the past eighty years, and the past twenty have been especially profound.

COMMUNICATION
Communication has quickly moved from all face-to-face and handwritten to mostly screen-to-screen. As a result, intimate face-to-face interaction has become less common and more awkward.

GRIEF CARE
We have moved from smaller and more intimate long-term support to public funerals with little long-term support. Quick and tragic news cycles have desensitized us to tragedy and suffering.

SENIOR CARE
This last century has seen a large shift from family-centered care to professional-centered care. For those who do stay with their families, the caregivers are so exhausted that sometimes little time is left for meaningful conversation. Underlying this, diminished vision, hearing, and memory can make interactions difficult.

MEDICAL CARE
Advances in all areas of healthcare, including mental healthcare, are allowing those with severe illness and injury to live longer, but chronic diseases, disabilities, and mental health issues make living more challenging.

SOCIAL CONNECTIONS
As centuries-old family and community bonds weaken, we become more dependent on online forums, schools, and workplaces to fill that social connection gap.

As these traditional forms of care have weakened, so have our human care skills.

When we consider just how quickly things have changed and continue to change, we can better grasp why so many of us are feeling the not-so-subtle shifts in loneliness, isolation, anxiety, depression, and emotional burnout.

As we compiled this information, an intern on the team, Byron, made the following observation: *"Everything I looked at—everything—has shifted away from being there for each other. We are distancing ourselves from everyone and everything. A great shift is happening, most linked to advancements in technology. What is astounding to me is how quickly everything is changing."*

Is it a coincidence that the mental health epidemic emerged in the middle of all of these other shifts?

TIMELINE OF HUMAN CARE

PRIOR TO 1900

COMMUNICATION

Communication is all face-to-face, verbal, or handwritten. The first telephone was invented in 1876.

GRIEF CARE

Families are responsible for burials. There is a recognized period of mourning.

SENIOR CARE

Seniors are cared for within family homes and supported by the community. Those without families are left to poorhouses.

MEDICAL CARE

A local doctor or families are the main source of healthcare. Some places have no doctor at all.

SOCIAL CONNECTIONS

People socialize with their families, closest neighbors, and houses of worship.

1900–1950

Communication is still mostly face-to-face, verbal, and handwritten; telephones are installed at a rapid pace. Phone booths and pay phones become available for those on the go.

Funeral homes start to spring up across the United States. World Wars start to desensitize an entire population to the grieving process.

Poorhouses decline. The Social Security Act is introduced in 1935, providing federal support and benefits for seniors.

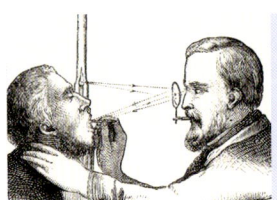

New medications to treat illnesses and alleviate pain begin to be developed. Access to hospitals greatly expands.

While families, neighbors, and religious establishments are still the main forms of socialization, schools and workplaces begin to enter the scene for social engagement.

TIMELINE IN PERSPECTIVE OF RECORDED HISTORY

3000 BC	2000 BC	1000 BC

How human care has changed over the last five thousand years

1950–2000   ## 2000–PRESENT

The following emerge at a rapid pace: dial phones, touch-tone phones, pagers, fax machines, five-pound mobile phones, flip phones, desktop computers, world wide web, and emails.

There is a shift away from face-to-face, one-to-one communication as handheld computers, smart phones, and social media emerge at a rapid pace.

 With the advent of television, cable news, violent movies, and video games, violence, dying, and death become commonplace in all forms of news and entertainment.

 Nonstop access to coverage of mass tragedies and constant updates on social media further desensitize us, creating a "move on" mentality to human pain, struggles, and grief.

Nursing homes, hospices, and assisted living care come on to the scene, providing support for seniors outside of our homes.

It is less common for families to care for seniors in their homes, as senior living facilities are the norm.

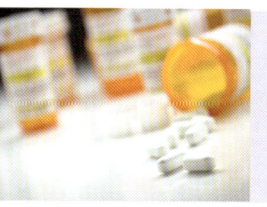 Life expectancy grows as advancements in medical care rise. The field of mental health emerges with new drugs being introduced for the first time for depression.

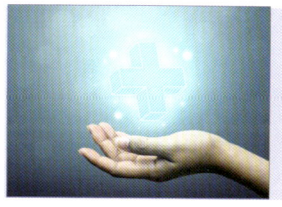 The Healthcare Revolution increases the burden of individuals needing to manage their own care. The Mental Health Epidemic and COVID-19 Pandemic emerge.

Easy air travel begins to split families. Dual-income and single-parent homes rise. As the pace of life increases, workplaces and schools start to become the main spaces where people socialize.

Social connections move online, families split farther apart, and religious affiliation declines. The workplace, schools, and hobbies emerge as this era's main face-to-face social centers.

0   1000 AD   1900 AD   TODAY

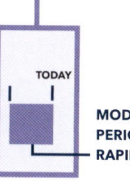

MODERN PERIOD OF RAPID CHANGE

When a Barn Burned

A look back on how we used to care for each other.

by Betty Reul

I grew up in wonderful rural Iowa in the 1940s and 50s. My parents owned a garage and filling station, which, together with a small grocery store/pub and the local creamery (where farmers brought their milk to be made into butter), was the hub of a farming community.

Family lived near, and neighbors were as important in our lives as family. We celebrated together, we worshipped together, and we shared joy and sadness together. We had many occasions to be together: birthdays, weddings, funerals, or just to have a good time!

Probably nothing brought the community together more than a disaster: tornado, fire, illness, or death. Barn fires were among the most devastating. At those times, the community really rallied. There was an urgency because not only was the family affected in distress, but their source of income was disrupted.

Because of the close relationships of the local people, getting help to those in need happened quite automatically. As soon as the news of the disaster was shared, usually through the local telephone switchboard, helping with the restoration was top priority.

Some would tend to the livestock and house them until the barn was rebuilt. Some would handle the razing and cleanup, while others offered needed support and comfort to the family. A new barn was built with the labor of the neighborhood. Everyone would prepare and bring food to the family and for those doing the physical work. It was the total focus of the community.

Having grown up in that environment, I find it concerning to see just how much our society has deviated from that today. Our dependence on each other has diminished. Younger generations have moved away from their home communities, neighbors are no longer critical for our well-being, and there's little time to entertain guests in our homes.

Each of the steps of progress has enabled us to be more independent and less dependent on others. But it has me wondering, at what cost? People's social and emotional needs are still the same. We still need to be there for each other.

WHY WE NEED COMFORT *NOW*

One hundred THOUSAND
annual drug overdose deaths in the US, a 28.5 percent increase in one year

26%
of adults in the United States suffer from a diagnosable mental illness

$225 BILLION
amount spent annually on mental health treatment and services

DEPRESSION ALONE IS ESTIMATED TO COST THE AMERICAN ECONOMY OVER 200 BILLION DOLLARS ANNUALLY.

—KESSLER, R. C.

*The Costs of Depression (2012)
Psychiatric Clinics of North America*

35%
increase in deaths by suicide in the US from 1999 to 2018

40 MILLION
adults in the US have an anxiety disorder (19 percent of the population)

61%
of young people aged eighteen to twenty-five in the US report feeling lonely frequently or all the time

WHERE WE ARE TODAY

Voices from the frontline that underscore the case for relearning the skill of comfort

CRISIS LINE DIRECTOR

Our understanding of why people suffer and the underlying causes of suffering has grown dramatically. Despite all this growth in knowledge, one thing remains the same. Connection and empathy are critical aspects of the human experience, and without them, people suffer.

As the director of a twenty-four-seven crisis center, I see the power of caring firsthand. In the fifty years since our crisis hotline started, the need has never declined and has grown exponentially. Over time pop culture has placed an emphasis on self-care and activities that people do alone. They try deep breathing, yoga, and long walks. For some, these coping skills are helpful, but what most people want is a caring human to be with them in their despair.

Breathing apps, coloring books, and walking can only provide so much comfort. People land in our crisis center, hurting, alone, and in need of caring others.

People do not call crisis hotlines because they need advice. They call because they need human care and connection. If we are to get serious about addressing the underlying pain that leads to so many challenges in people's lives, we must go back to the human foundation, which is caring and comforting one another. We have so much work to do, and it all starts with comfort.

> "People do not call crisis hotlines because they need advice. They call because they need human care and connection."

Laura Mayer is the Director of PRS CrisisLink, Washington DC

FEELING DIFFERENT THAN EVERYONE ELSE

When I was a child back in Australia, I was the only nonwhite student in my class. I always felt different but tried my best to roll with the punches. When people would look at me differently or when teachers would call me racial slurs, I thought that was normal. Because I was taught to just do my best as a student and not make excuses for myself, I just accepted this reality.

When I moved to the United States in middle school, I found it difficult to fit in again. On top of the social anxiety, I also faced a lot of academic anxiety. I didn't know how to study for tests, felt overwhelmed by my classes, and felt that everyone was so much more advanced than me. I felt left behind academically and socially.

Eventually, I decided I'd had enough of feeling isolated and wrote a suicide note. At the time, I was living in Richmond, Virginia, and didn't have an academic institution I felt proud of. I had no clear sense of identity, and it felt like no one really knew I existed. What kind of value could I bring to anybody? The one thing that stopped me from following through with suicide was a phone call from my friend Johnny. He was one of the last people I thought would ever call me, but he told me he hoped we could hang out soon and that he'd love to throw me a party the next time I came up to Northern Virginia. I was taken aback, but I agreed, and Johnny ultimately did throw me a party where I wound up meeting many of the people I now consider my closest friends.

Through the support of these friends, I learned the value of being vulnerable about my struggles and creating a space for others to be vulnerable with me. I've learned how critical it is to know how to comfort and support each other. You don't have to pry into each other's problems or force each other into saying anything. You just have to be patient and understanding and create an environment where people feel comfortable opening up on their own time. As insecure as I initially was, being vulnerable about my experiences with depression has helped me realize I'm not alone.

I wouldn't have learned these key lessons if it weren't for that phone call from Johnny. He's like a brother to me now, and I don't know that he'll ever know how much that phone call meant to me.

> *"As insecure as I initially was, being vulnerable about my experiences with depression has helped me realize I'm not alone."*

Matthew Henry is an Author and TEDx Speaker

37

PERSPECTIVES FROM A TEACHER

Our students today live in a world of constant media influence. I teach students who look at the perfect world created in magazines, television shows, and social media. I teach early elementary students who are dressed like fashion models and sneak makeup to school. I teach students who think reality television is real. I teach students who smile on the outside but have immense internal sadness. I teach students ostracized by their friends on social media. I teach students of all ages who are considering suicide, seeing it as their only option to end loneliness or bullying. I teach students scarred by the trauma they have seen or experienced firsthand. I teach students who do not know how to communicate with each other. I teach students who do self-harm. I teach students who appear to not care about anything.

NAVIGATING IDENTITY

From a young age, I started exhibiting strange behaviors and "compulsions." Around the same time, I also started experiencing same-sex attraction, a realization I suppressed until I couldn't be in denial any longer. I couldn't rationalize parts of myself but didn't know how to explain things. My OCD and sexuality were two aspects I had no context for in the world around me.

> "I teach students of all ages who are considering suicide, seeing it as their only option to end loneliness or bullying."

Julie Wall teaches art to students age four to sixty-plus.

> "What I needed from the people in my life was not questions but care and comfort. True care begins with not questioning another person's experience, even if it doesn't make sense to us."

Kelly Shannon is Inspiring Comfort's Marketing and Sales Manager

When I began voicing what I was experiencing, people started asking me questions. While I knew most of these questions were being asked with good intentions, usually, they only made me feel more emotionally exhausted than I already was. I didn't want to explain over and over again why what I was experiencing was valid and real. Most of the time, I just wanted to feel held.

What I needed from the people in my life was not questions but care and comfort. True care begins with not questioning another person's experience, even if it doesn't make sense to us.

This has made me feel held. The best friend who sat on the floor with me, not needing to speak, just being there, while I cried. The mom who called and sent a thoughtful card after a particularly hard therapy session that said, "I'm so proud of you."

The littlest actions from the people who show up day after day are what make all the difference.

PSYCHOTHERAPIST VIEW

For over twenty years, I have been a psychotherapist in private practice. I have seen the rise of a significant problem that continues to worsen. That problem is disconnection, loneliness, and social isolation. In the past two decades, technology and social media have drastically changed the ways that people communicate and connect. Human relationships—whether friendships, intimate relationships, or affiliations with groups—have become cyber relationships. While this can have positive effects, it can also become very isolating.

Human beings crave touch and real-life companionship. Studies show how brain chemistry is positively affected by physical touch with another living being. As human beings, we are programmed to be in relationships. I believe we can make a significant impact by intentionally connecting and providing constructive, real-life companionship. This kind of companionship is soothing, healing, and therapeutic. Not only that, this kind of connection also helps us to be better humans by fostering love, compassion, and empathy.

> "In the past two decades, technology and social media have drastically changed the ways that people communicate and connect. Human relationships—whether they are friendships, intimate relationships, or affiliations with groups—have become cyber relationships."

Daniel E. Mattila, M.Div., LCSW in Private Practice

THE DANGERS OF ISOLATION

"I could not reach out. I needed someone to reach in. If just one person had shown me an ounce of care, I would not have jumped off that bridge." —K. Hines

THE NEED FOR "OTHERS CARE"

My youngest daughter, Audrey, was a junior in high school when the pandemic hit. School went online, and in the beginning, she felt freedom and fun in learning from her bedroom. It was supposed to only last a few weeks, then a few months, and then longer and longer and longer. When she graduated over a year later, she sat with classmates that she had barely seen in person for fifteen months.

Three months later, it was time to drop her off at college nine hours away from home. Something was far different from the drop-offs for our older two daughters during their college years, and it wasn't only because Audrey is our baby.

The pandemic isolated Audrey from her friends for eighteen months, but Audrey's generation is also the first generation to make and maintain friendships through a screen. Her first phone was a smartphone, which meant she monitored friend groups and activities twenty-four-seven from the start. The difference in social interaction in her generation compared with my older two daughters, who didn't have smartphones until they were older, is palpable.

There is a reason it was the hardest of goodbyes, and there is a reason we need to show more support and care to our students than ever before. Let's add coworkers, parents, friends, neighbors, relatives, strangers, and those we disagree with to the list.

Between the forced separation from a pandemic and the societal shift of "screen separation," we have been spending far more time alone. Additionally, one of the most heavily discussed solutions to the stress from all of this is "self-care," which is needed and good, but it often entails more time alone.

If we focus too much on self, our relationships get out of balance and our interest in human connection can decrease when it might be what we need most.

43

IT WILL TAKE ALL OF US

THE NEW LEADERSHIP SKILL

Has an over-reliance on technology caused some of our current mental health epidemic? The answer is a resounding yes. Can we rely on technology alone to fix what is broken? The answer is a resounding no. Solutions that place people behind a screen will continue to add to the awkwardness of being together in person. Please refer back to the last section if you need examples.

We are human beings—multi-dimensional, emotional, and complicated. As much as artificial intelligence and the use of screens are growing and taking over our world, they can never take over our humanity. We need each other, including all of the sights and sounds and feelings that go with being in person with each other.

Who is responsible for nurturing this care, and where do we apply it? The answer is everyone and everywhere.

Our homes, our parents, and our tight-knit communities have traditionally been the place where these skills were nurtured, but that can no longer be the only case. Here is why:

- There is not equity in that approach. Not everyone has a caring environment around them.
- Families are moving apart from each other and splitting up at a record pace.
- Our diverse society requires us to care for every single person, regardless of their skin color, ethnicity, socioeconomic status, sexual identity, political affiliation, religion, or personality.
- We have a much faster pace of life with far more stress than any other time in human history.
- Our divided and hurting world needs mending in every setting where people gather.

I recently worked with a group of education professionals who were feeling emotionally exhausted. When the data from their pre-surveys came in, it was clear why:

71%
were feeling anxiety and/or depression.

80%
did not feel seen or cared for in their jobs.

35%
did not feel cared for outside of work.

Let those numbers sink in. Over a third of this group had no tribe–nowhere to feel cared for.

What happens when we don't reach individuals feeling this way? Think about that.
In this new world, if you do not know how to show care, you will not be a good leader, a good friend, a good partner, a good professor, a good doctor, a good lawyer, a good anything.

Let's go.

47

"The Awkward Zone™ is the place where you want to help a person who is struggling but don't know what to say or do."

PART TWO

THE PROCESS

What Stops Us

The Awkward Zone

The Process and the Science

The Mindset and the Choice

Who Needs Care

WHY WE DON'T COMFORT: WE'VE ALL BEEN THERE

What happens when we are caught off guard and don't know what to do?

THE SUPERMARKET

The scene takes place every day in supermarkets across America. On one end of the store, someone walks in who wishes more than anything they didn't have to be out in public, but they must eat. For the sake of an example, we'll call this person Jane. She unexpectedly lost her husband and doesn't want to talk to anyone. Jane is desperate to get through the store without running into people she knows. She's hurting, grieving, lonely, traumatized, and depressed.

On the other end of the store enters Suzie. She's in a hurry and has exactly eight minutes to get the ten things on her list before picking up her son from soccer. Jane and Suzie know each other, but it's been a while since they've spoken. Somewhere midstore, they turn the corner and find themselves in the same aisle.

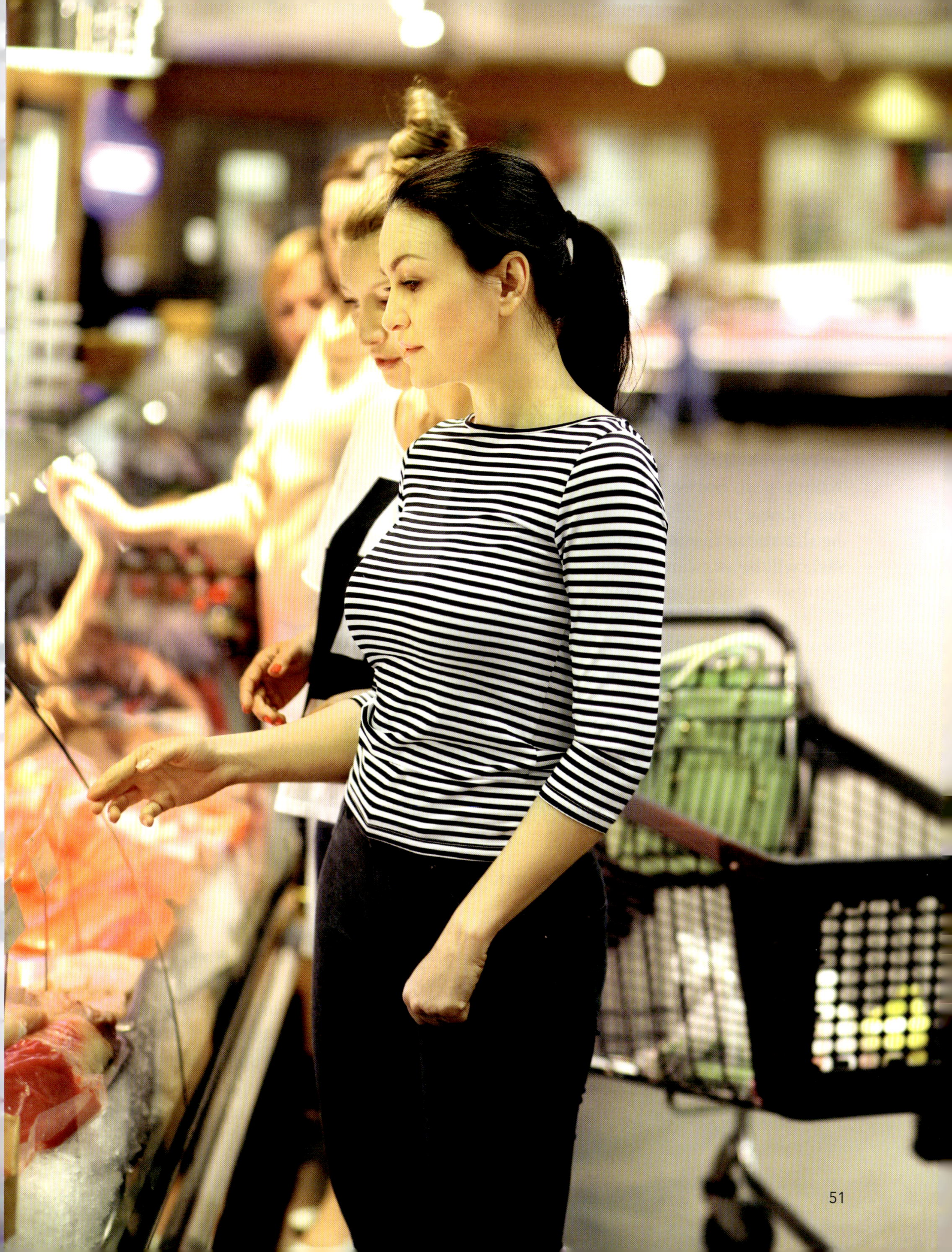

WHAT STOPS US? THE AWKWARD ZONE™

"This is an actual thing! Finally, there is a name for what we are all feeling."

—FIRST-YEAR COLLEGE STUDENT LEARNING ABOUT THE AWKWARD ZONE.

During some recent programming we conducted among first-year university students, they were put in small groups and asked to discuss what stops them from showing care to each other. I jumped into one of these groups with eight students as they talked about their personal comfort assessment data.

Empathy and compassion were important to them, and they rated themselves high on the ability to see those who were struggling. However, on the flip side of that, they were all feeling like no one saw them when they struggled. How can that happen?

None of them wanted to be the friend who appeared not to care, but they got stuck. It was awkward. They didn't want to say or do the wrong thing.

When I asked them, "Is this resonating with you?" one of the students looked up at me and said, "Oh my gosh, yes! This is an actual thing! Finally, there is a name for what we are all feeling. It is indeed the Awkward Zone. Thank you."

Countless thoughts, behaviors, and emotions stop us from showing care. We can have the best intentions and feel loads of empathy and compassion, but if we don't address the emotions and behaviors that get in our way of acting, we will never begin to mend our hurting world.

It has never been more challenging to know what to say and do when those around us are struggling. Think back to the timeline and also to just living in the past decade. We are far more aware of the cultural and racial differences in the world around us and are therefore more sensitive to our words and actions. We are also dealing with more ideological divisions than we can count: politics, the pandemic, religion, schooling, healthcare, you name it. At times it seems like we are disagreeing more than agreeing with each other on anything. All of these factors get in the way of showing care.

The good news is when we focus on the singular task of caring for someone, none of these differences and divisions should matter. When our goal is to help someone feel seen, heard, understood, and cared for, differences and divisions don't come into play; they fall away.

Breaking through this Awkward Zone™ could be the very thing needed to mend these growing chasms.

WHERE TO BEGIN

It starts with the basic understanding that everyone needs and deserves the support and care of those around them. As we have learned, we are wired for human connection, and it's essential for our well-being.

Because of this, plus the fact that those struggling may be deep in the pit and unable to reach out for help, we begin with two mindset barriers that need to be fully banished:

"Some people don't deserve to be cared for."

"It's up to the one struggling to ask for help."

Please don't let these thoughts enter your mind. We then need to add in an inconvenient truth.

"Hurting people hurt people."

Always remember that some of the most hurtful things are said in the midst of the worst challenges. It takes a strong heart to see through this and understand that care might be the only thing to stop the cycle.

In other words, never give up. Maybe through repeated acts of care, hearts will open and change.

THE AWKWARD ZONE™

While researching and observing care behaviors over the past ten years, identifiable patterns emerged that could help us understand what is stopping us from supporting each other. Because these are behaviors and not personality traits, we may find ourselves in any of these buckets at different points in our lives. The goal here is to be able to recognize our own barriers at any given time so we can apply the strategies and tools in the rest of this book to break through this Awkward Zone™.

MINDSET BARRIERS

The first barriers happen when we "hear of" or "know of" someone struggling and fail to act. It could be someone in our organization, or class, or a family member or friend. If we fail to reach out to support them, we will either be a doubter or a deflector.

DOUBTERS

When hearing of someone struggling doubters will allow awkwardness, fear, regret, and insecurity to interfere with taking action.

The belief: I don't know how to help.

The reality: There are evidence-based tools and strategies you can use to support someone struggling.

DEFLECTORS

When deflectors hear of someone struggling, they don't want to "go there". They may think it's a burden, or it's not their place or that others will cover it.

The belief: It's not my place or the right time to get involved.

The reality: Even if you barely know the person, it *is* your place & small actions will go a long way.

RESPONDING BARRIERS

Regardless of our mindset barriers, we all end up face to face with people struggling and will be caught off guard on what to say or do. It could be in the supermarket, on an elevator or anywhere people gather. In this situation, if you fail to adequately support the person, it will be because you are either a fixer or an avoider.

FIXERS

When face to face with someone struggling, fixers jump in but can stumble because they are not confident about what to say and do. Fixers don't love silence and want to find solutions.

The belief: I can help by giving advice or telling them what helped me.

The reality: People struggling are usually not looking for advice — they need to be acknowledged and validated.

AVOIDERS

When face to face with someone struggling, avoiders will shy away from bringing it up. They are uncomfortable and will leave that elephant smack dab in the middle of the room.

The belief: I'll avoid the situation so I don't do anything wrong.

The reality: Caring for others is not difficult and is critical for our own well-being.

MINDSET BARRIER BEHAVIORS

If you know of someone struggling and fail to act, which of these ten behaviors are you are most guilty of? Do you rate yourself a doubter or deflector?

1. FEAR
The biggest barrier. Fear of more pain or rejection. "I'm afraid I'll _____," so I don't say/do anything.

2. IT'S AWKWARD
I don't know what to say or do. It makes me uncomfortable.

3. SOMEONE ELSE
Can do this better than me and will handle it. I'm not wired to do this.

4. I'VE DONE ALL I CAN
I've reached the end of my helping rope.

5. IT'S NOT MY BUSINESS
It's not my place to step into the situation.

6. I'M STRUGGLING TOO
I can't take on their burden. I've done all I can, and I just don't have time.

7. THEY APPEAR OKAY
They must be over it, and if I bring it up, I might make them upset.

8. YOU KNOW HIM BETTER
I'll ask friends how someone is doing instead of reaching out myself.

9. REGRET
I didn't do anything. It's too late now. I'm embarrassed, and I wish I had done something sooner.

10. IT'S HARD TO RELATE TO THEM
They have different lifestyles and beliefs than I do. I may offend them.

RESPONDING BARRIER BEHAVIORS

When you run into someone unexpectedly who you know to be struggling, which of these ten behaviors are you are most guilty of? Do you rate yourself a fixer or an avoider?

1. LET ME KNOW
I will ask them to "let me know what you need" without having anything specific in mind.

2. THE CHEERLEADER
I will try to cheer them up.

3. THIS HELPED ME
I will try to help them by telling them what helped me.

4. NERVOUS CHATTER
I want to help but, in my nervousness, I talk too much.

5. I'M HURTING TOO
I will share my own problems so they know that we all hurt, and I sympathize with them.

6. ELEPHANT IN THE ROOM

I will make small talk but avoid the subject because I don't want to upset them.

7. I MOVE ON

I have been known to be there for someone at the beginning of their crisis but never follow up.

8. NOT GOING THERE

I don't know what to say, so I avoid them all together by walking the other way.

9. THEY'RE OVER IT

When you've reached the end of your helping rope. "I just don't know what to do anymore. It's been so long, and I've tried everything to help them. I'm exhausted, and I just don't feel like helping anymore."

10. IT'S ALL MY FAULT

I will apologize profusely for not touching base sooner and talk about all the reasons why.

THE CIRCLE OF COMFORT AND THE SCIENCE BEHIND IT

The Ultimate Skill of Human Connection: You simply cannot comfort someone without connecting with them in a caring way.

Let's take a look at the process we developed at Inspiring Comfort for learning this critical skill through Sam's story.

FROM APATHY TO COMFORT

Sam was a sixth-grader who didn't much like being at school. He didn't have friends in his class and spent most of his time with his aide. After school, he preferred to go straight home and play video games. He definitely had no interest in joining an after-school club. However, his grandmother, whom he lived with, had other ideas. She signed Sam up to attend Project Comfort.

Sam was not only extremely uninterested in this, but he was downright combative. He disrupted the first session shouting out things like, "This is stupid," "I don't even want to be here," and "I don't care about this." His aide, a wonderful woman who went to each class with him every day, came to his side and encouraged him to stay, but he was getting more and more agitated, and it was becoming awkward for everyone. She whispered they would be leaving early but would be back for the next session.

During the second session, Sam again sat outside of the circle with his arms crossed. He had a few outbursts, but he stayed, watched with his arms still crossed, and participated in the activity. Together with his aide, he identified someone who was in need of care, thought of what to say to them, and made a beautiful comfort plaque to be hand-delivered.

By the fourth session, Sam sat with the group in the circle. He didn't say much, but his arms were no longer crossed, and even better, he had followed through on his in-session and take-home tasks since the second session.

By the fifth session, Sam walked into the classroom and asked if it was Project Comfort day. When he was told yes, he said, "Good."

By the seventh session, when the following question was posed to the group during that day's lesson: "How would you feel if you didn't get to see your family for a long time?" Sam raised his hand and answered, "Sad, disappointed, discouraged."

By the eighth session, Sam arrived early and helped sort out the activity supplies. That was a wow. In this final session, students were prompted to think of people who help them but may not feel appreciated. After several students didn't quite hit the mark with their answers, Sam suggested the custodian at his school—a perfect answer. That's who he chose to comfort that day.

Witnessing Sam move from combative to attentive to participating to initiating was one of the most amazing progressions I have ever witnessed in a withdrawn and isolated child—all in eight short weeks. How could that happen?

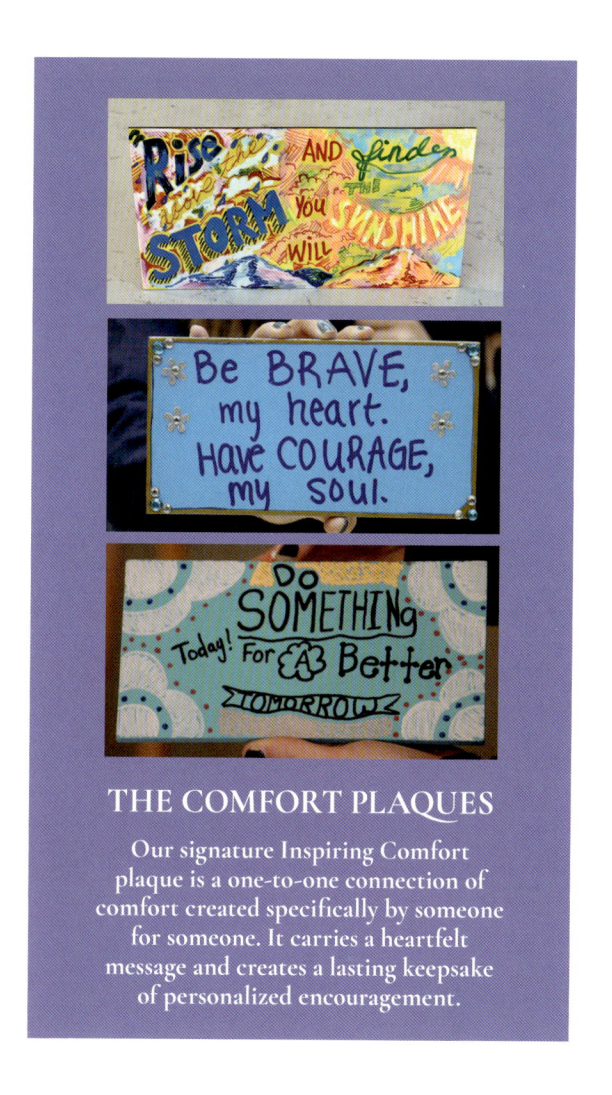

THE COMFORT PLAQUES

Our signature Inspiring Comfort plaque is a one-to-one connection of comfort created specifically by someone for someone. It carries a heartfelt message and creates a lasting keepsake of personalized encouragement.

Research Pilot

An open pilot study of the Inspiring Comfort program, Project Comfort was conducted with adolescents from a middle school in New York City. Initial findings showed that teenagers who completed the Inspiring Comfort program reported reductions in loneliness and depressive symptoms, along with increases in compassion for others and self-compassion. In addition, all students expressed that they would recommend the program to a peer. When asked what they learned from the program, students highlighted skills for how to be a better listener, better care for others, and be more kind to others. (Fox, Walls, Thomas, Marr, Breux, and Masia, in preparation)

THE CIRCLE OF COMFORT

Learning how to care for and support others requires intentional connection.

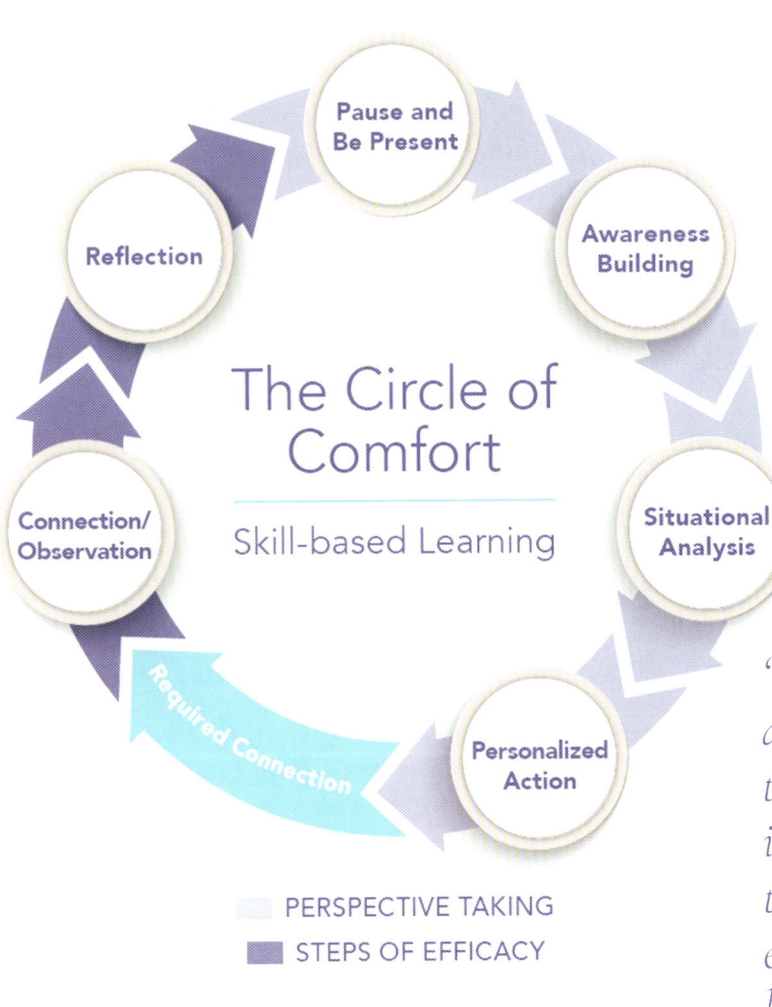

The Circle of Comfort
Skill-based Learning

- Pause and Be Present
- Awareness Building
- Situational Analysis
- Personalized Action
- Required Connection
- Connection/Observation
- Reflection

▢ PERSPECTIVE TAKING
▪ STEPS OF EFFICACY

"What I value so much about this approach to teaching comfort as a skill is its step-by-step focus on teaching skills to enhance empathy and removing barriers that inhibit it, all in a science backed way."

—Dr. David DeSteno, Psychology Professor at Northeastern University, Inspiring Comfort's Scientific Advisor

When practiced, specific steps equip people with this skill of connection and care. It's simply impossible to comfort someone if you don't connect with them. We saw at the start how Sam was feeling only apathy, but over the course of eight sessions, when required to give comfort, empathy and compassion emerged. He was able to cultivate these critical emotions with continued actions.

The Circle of Comfort works with all personality types and in all situations where people are needing care and support.

When this process is repeated again and again, trust builds and relationships grow.

PAUSE AND BE PRESENT—We begin by removing other distractions so we can help those who are suffering. For people of faith, this is also where prayer resides. Becoming still in the moment, pausing, and being present.

AWARENESS BUILDING—We take time to look up from our devices to see those around us who are in need of support. It's equally important to keep remembering those we already know to be struggling and continue to walk with them in their pain.

SITUATIONAL ANALYSIS—We must analyze their situation before deciding how to help. We consider what they need and what they enjoy—what words or actions they would like from us.

PERSONALIZED ACTION—We select an expression of "just for you" care. A call, text, card, meal, book, social outing, or dropping off their favorite treat. Countless things can be done, and the accumulation of these actions ultimately brings a deep and trusting relationship.

CONNECTION—The key to the skill of comfort is this intentional step. If no connection, no comfort. In this step, we put all focus on the person we are helping. We offer our hearts, ears, friendship, and time. The person who is being comforted will feel seen and encouraged, given a bit of hope.

REFLECTION—We reflect back on how much this connection has meant for both the giver and receiver of comfort. The skill of comfort brings care to both parties. Another marble is put into the marble jar. Trust is growing, and the relationship is deepening. At the end of this reflection is the time to determine what the next expression of care should be, so the circle can begin again.

TAKEAWAY

When we are hurting—when we have hard stuff in our life—this is the perfect medicine for giving ourselves some hope. We can reach out and connect with someone else who is going through a tough time. It's counterintuitive, actually, as sometimes we look at this as extra "work" that we don't have time for. But by helping others, we will help ourselves. Every time.

That is a circle of comfort: you to someone, someone back to you.

THE SECOND CIRCLE

*The only hurts that don't heal
 are the ones we don't share.*

Think back to the section on the dangers of isolation and how we need each other. Completing the care cycle means it's not enough to just give comfort. We also need to know how to receive it. This can be really hard, especially for those who want to handle things on their own and don't like to bring others into their problems. But hard times can have a way of bringing reality crashing down on us until we become vulnerable enough to acknowledge our need for it.

BE COMFORTED

Opening your heart to receive comfort completes the sphere of comfort. The combination of the circles makes us whole.

1. Remove distractions, pause, and be present.

2. Find gratitude for the person who wants to care for you.

3. Consider that everyone has different strengths in caring for each other, but the intentions are good.

4. Help them help you. Let them know what your emotional needs are.

5. Open your heart to their care and connection.

6. Reflect back on how the process is helping both of you.

I have just the story to share that will demonstrate this to you.

It's a story of two Phillips who share a tragic connection. Both Phillips lost their sons to suicide, six weeks apart from each other.

Phillip Tyler, a security officer at Gonzaga University, was there to help Phillip Martin collect his son's belongings after his son Chris died by suicide as a junior at Gonzaga.

Six weeks later, his own son Devon took his life. Prior to this, Phillip Tyler was active in many circles but was seen as professional and polished. It was uncharacteristic of him to be openly vulnerable. His wife encouraged him to reach out to Phillip Martin, and so he did.

Phillip Martin, knowing this grief himself, knew he didn't have to say much. Listening was most important. But what he did say was: "It's okay to cry, Phil. It's okay to let go of the grief. It's okay to let go of that guilt. That doesn't mean you're forgetting about it. That means you're freeing yourself from the pain so you can go forward."

For Phillip Tyler, this conversation was one he'll always remember. "It opened up a sense of vulnerability and comfort that I thought wasn't there for many years. I cried. And Phil cried. And we had this beautiful conversation. And to this day, he calls. He checks in. He texts. We share messages back and forth on holidays and on our children's birthdays. That was a lesson I had to learn as an adult parent from another parent, another adult who had suffered loss, but never judged me for the way I felt about it. Phil taught me that it was okay to be vulnerable. Phil taught me what comfort was. That's why he is such a dear friend."

Both Phillips, developing a deep, lasting friendship, learned that in both the giving and receiving of comfort, we learn how to move forward. Being willing to comfort each other through their grief was the basis of the amazing friendship they share today. That is the essence of both giving and receiving comfort.

THE SCIENCE BEHIND THE SKILL
FIVE QUESTIONS WITH DR. DAVID DESTENO

A sit-down with Dr. David DeSteno, professor of psychology at Northeastern University, and a fellow at the American Psychological Association.

How is Comfort an evidence-based skill?

Most of us think we're compassionate. We think we'd step up to help someone in need when the time came. But scientific research shows time and again that people's beliefs about how they'll treat others doesn't often match their actions. When it comes to offering comfort, evidence matters. Questionnaires about what people intend to do don't mean much. What's convincing is seeing behaviors actually change, seeing people take the initiative to reach out to help others in ways that can be difficult at times. Ways that are personal, that have connection, not just spending a few dollars and moving on. What impresses me about the work of Inspiring Comfort is the changes those who have gone through it report. They're spending time to connect with others, to have difficult conversations, to be there in ways that aren't always easy to do.

In helping others, how are we helped?

For scientists, this has long been a question: Why should we help other people if it is difficult or costs us time, money, or other resources? The problem with that view is it betrays ignorance of the fact that humans are a social species. Over time, we gain from helping each other. Yes, it can be costly to go help someone in the short term. Even giving them a shoulder to cry on can be difficult to handle emotionally. But time and again, research shows those small costs tend to be repaid in greater amounts over time. When adversity strikes (and adversity always does), those who have extended compassion to others have a community ready and willing to support them in their own time of need. Building these social networks is so important to our well-being that our brains actually value giving help to others. When we do it, the brain's reward centers activate. Why? Because enhancing others' well-being is a down payment on enhancing our own.

Can you learn comfort even if you don't feel empathy or compassion in your heart?

Yes! And this is an extremely important fact to understand. Empathy and compassion are usually not innate. In fact, great research by a psychologist named Jamil Zaki at Stanford shows simply getting people to believe they can improve their empathy immediately makes them more willing to comfort others. What I value so much about this approach to teaching comfort as a skill is its step-by-step focus on teaching skills to enhance empathy and removing barriers that inhibit it, all in a science backed way. One of the biggest reasons people don't engage in the sometimes-difficult work of comforting others is that they feel ill-equipped. Teaching them how to deal with potentially awkward situations, how to reach out to others, how to step up and simply be there when needed can help them to feel efficacious. And decades of research shows that feelings of efficaciousness are one of the biggest predictors for whether someone will engage in an activity. To try and do something challenging, we have to feel we have the tools. And the programs and workshops Inspiring Comfort is building, including this book, are built around exactly that: giving people the tools they need to comfort others.

Why is it important to focus on a specific person to help while learning comfort instead of sending something randomly?

For most of our evolutionary history, humans interacted face-to-face. There was no internet; there was no Amazon. We couldn't simply hit a button to send some money or a

> "Enhancing others' wellbeing is a down payment on enhancing our own."

teddy bear to children in need. So now, when we attempt to comfort others in this way, there's a big miscalibration and motivation problem. Without truly coming to know the person we're trying to comfort, it's difficult to know what they truly need. Backing up the point, a good deal of research shows that the help and gifts people most appreciate aren't a function of cost but rather a function of thought. Did someone spend the time to figure out what I need? If so, it is very affirming and comforting. If not, it's a throw-a-way. But an even bigger problem than miscalibration is motivation. When we send twenty dollars or a stuffed animal by clicking a button, we lose that personal interaction. When I mentioned above that our brains' reward circuits are attuned to giving to others, that means giving in a way where this a social interaction—a way where we can see the joy and comfort those sacrifices bring to the people we're trying to help. If we don't get that feedback, it can become difficult to keep on comforting. For these reasons, I would urge people, at least at the start, to focus on helping individuals with whom they can interact. That's the way to train your brain, so to speak, to learn the value that is intrinsic to comforting others.

Is it good for us to focus on helping someone else through their struggles even when we have our own?

Yes, but with a caveat. My research group has been investigating this question for a while. In work led by my colleague Daniel Lim, we find those who have suffered their own adversities in life and successfully come through them are more ready to offer comfort to others. In fact, one primary reason why they do so is that they feel they know how to help. Having lived through adversity themselves, they realize how important receiving comfort from others was to them and how even seemingly small acts can make an important difference. This work suggests that focusing on teaching comforting skills is essential. For those who have been fortunate enough not to have faced significant adversity in their lives, learning the comforting skills that others have developed via more trying experiences can be a major step in enabling their ability to empathize. But now for the caveat. It can be difficult to comfort others when you're in the throes of distress yourself. When you're suffering, let others comfort you. It's important to remember that when it comes to the circle of comfort, being willing to accept is as important as being willing to give. Along the road of life, sometimes people need to do one or the other. The trick to living a good life is to be able to do both.

Dr. David DeSteno is a professor of psychology at Northeastern University and the author of Emotional Success: The Power of Gratitude, Compassion, and Pride.

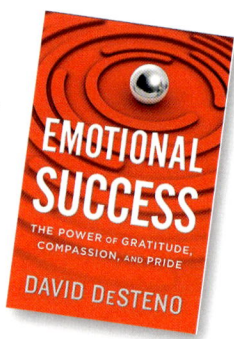

The Scientific Benefits of Comfort

FIVE KEY TAKEAWAYS FROM DR. DAVID DESTENO

Mutual Benefits

Enhancing others' well-being is a down payment on enhancing our own.

Learning Empathy

Comfort can be learned even in those who lack empathy.

Thoughtful Gifts

Research indicates that the help and gifts people most appreciate aren't a function of cost but rather a function of thought.

Personal Interaction

DeSteno urges people to focus on helping individuals with whom they can interact. People can train their brain to learn the intrinsic value of comforting others.

Recieving Comfort

Being willing to accept comfort is as important as being willing to give it. Along the road of life, sometimes people need to do one or the other. The trick to living a good life is to be able to do both.

THE CORE OF OUR HUMANITY: WHAT'S REALLY GOING ON

You meet thousands of people and none of them really touch you. And then you meet one person and your life is changed forever.—Unknown.

When we think back to the story of Sam, a backstory needs to be told.

Sam came into that group beaten down and hurting. He no longer lives with his mom, who has a history of mental illness or his sister who is often hospitalized with addiction struggles. Because of this instability, Sam lives full time with his grandma, who is doing the very best she can. He has difficulty regulating his emotions and filtering his thoughts and words. He goes through his school day with an assigned aide in an attempt to help him get through the day and stay in class.

Having difficulty with emotions and being prone to verbal outbursts, Sam is left without a friend group—isolated, sad, frustrated, and angry. You can imagine the gremlins he faces in his head each and every minute of each and every day.

Like so many in our world today who feel like they have no place where they really belong or are lacking purpose, Sam needed to feel like he belonged as a first step. In order for him to progress from combative to attentive to participating to initiating, he needed a place where:

- He felt safe to participate.
- People would appreciate him for who he was.
- His input would be valued by everyone present.
- He felt cared for.

CORE HUMAN TRUTHS

Relational needs are at the core of our humanity. They are the foundation of every relationship and every interaction we have with each other. Every single person we interact with, on every level:

* Safety

* Belonging

* Understanding

* Trust

* Relationships

* Community

* Encouragement

Needs to be:

* Valued

* Heard

* Assured of Hope

None of these things can be accomplished alone. We need each other.

IT STARTS WITH THE RIGHT MINDSET

"To add value to others, one must first value others."

–JOHN MAXWELL

While we were developing our Inspiring Comfort programming, it was critical for us to create an environment where everyone can thrive, especially people like Sam, who start with only apathy in their hearts. The foundation must be grounded in human values; an atmosphere of trust, security, and belonging.

With that in mind, all programming we do begins with reviewing the right mindset needed to show care. In our youth programming, we call these our Comfort, Care and Connection Rules and Guidelines and require students to review them at the beginning of every session together.

The great truth here is that regardless of the emotions we are feeling, we can follow a process to show care. This, in turn, results in someone being grateful for what we did while we feel satisfied that we helped another person.

This is what happened with Sam. He agreed to these principles on day one and reread them at the start of each session, allowing his walls to gradually break down.

Putting others before ourselves allows these positive emotions to be cultivated, which is truly the best self-care of all.

THE SHOWING UP MINDSET

WE REMOVE DISTRACTIONS
We calm our inner chatter, exhale and become present in the moment.

WE BELONG
No one is unworthy. We share the common goals of mending our world and ourselves through care and connection.

WE GENUINELY CARE
This may sound simple but it's not. We reach into our heart, not our brain. We know that every person we know is dealing with more than we know and people will know it when we truly show care.

WE HAVE GRATITUDE
No matter how hard life gets, when we bring care, we will improve the lives of others plus our own life. We smile and show how appreciative we are for this time together.

WE DON'T JUDGE
We will affirm, validate and acknowledge the pain in others and care for them even if we don't share the same lifestyle or belief system.

WE CHOOSE OTHERS
We can spend our lives focused on ourselves and our needs, or we can choose to help others. The truth is, when we help others, we help ourselves. So that's what we do.

WE ALLOW PEOPLE IN
We allow others to care for us. We need each other.

WE TAKE PRIDE
We take ownership of this process and our goals. If we are ridiculed or some do not agree with us, we will not engage. Instead we will stand up for what is right, knowing that this is a lifestyle we have chosen for the long term.

WE ACCEPT MISTAKES
We've all messed up – no one is perfect. We've all done things we regret and here we will start fresh, looking ahead to all of the good that we can do.

WE TRUST
Every day with every person we interact with, we have a choice. We can assume the best in that person, or we can assume the worst. It's not ok to assume the worst in someone, so here we will trust and assume the best.

WHAT GOES ON WHEN WE COMFORT

When we want to comfort someone, we start here. We focus on them and not us. And at some point, the receiver of comfort will become a giver of comfort, and a new circle of comfort begins.

THE GIVER OF COMFORT

1. Is intentional in looking to see the basic human needs of a person

2. Is focused on the needs of the other

3. Is concentrating on saying or doing something that will bring this person comfort

4. Is aware in seeing what more this person might need

5. Is feeling comforted by comforting someone as their empathic system engages

6. Is reflecting more and more that life is not about *me*

7. Is realizing that a friendship is beginning or is deepening

THE RECEIVER OF COMFORT

1. Feels acknowledged and validated

2. Feels seen and loved

3. Feels encouragement

4. Feels understood

5. Feels a sense of belonging and a sense of safety

6. Over time, will recognize a trust and a peace in the presence of this person

7. Feels a deeper connection or friendship with this person

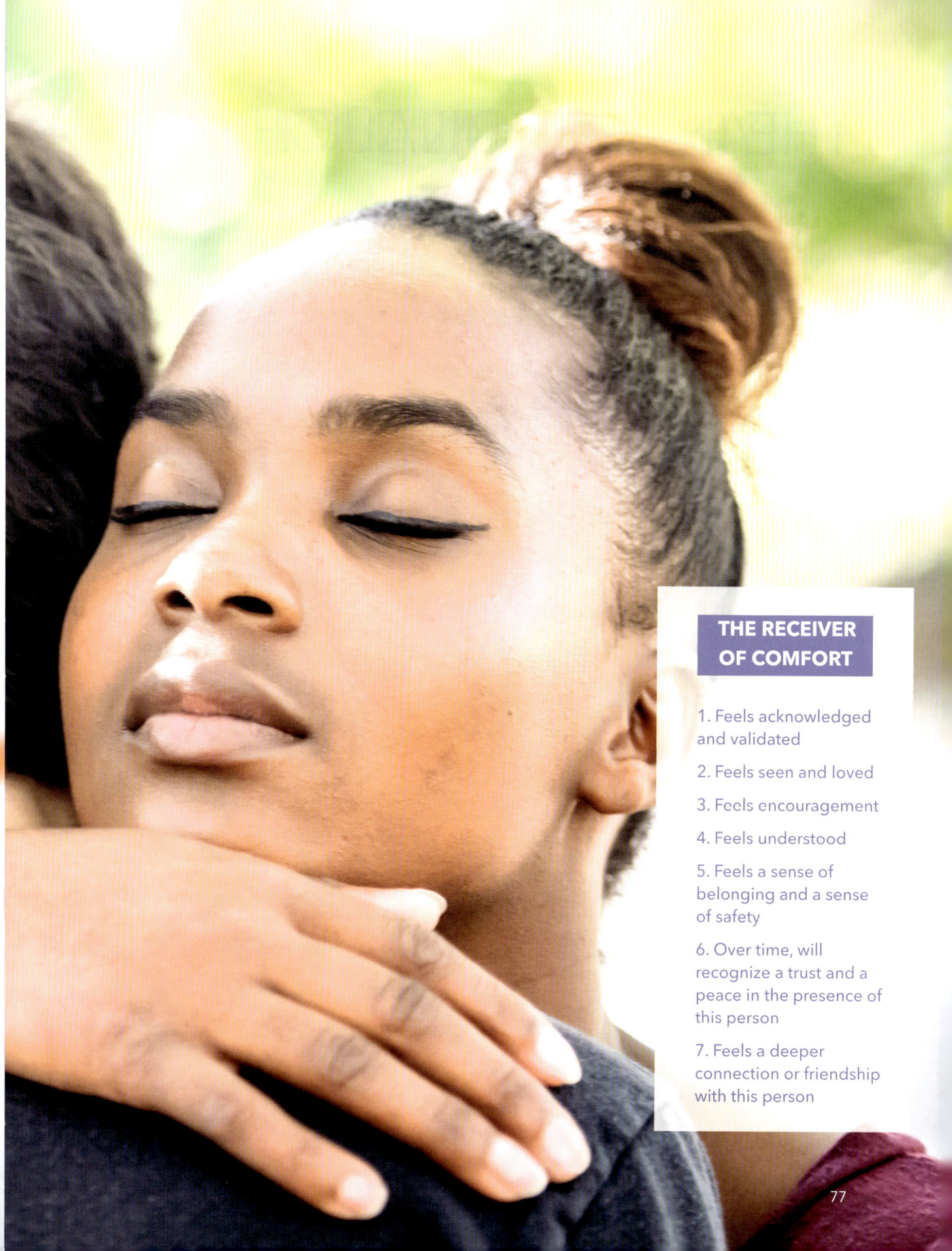

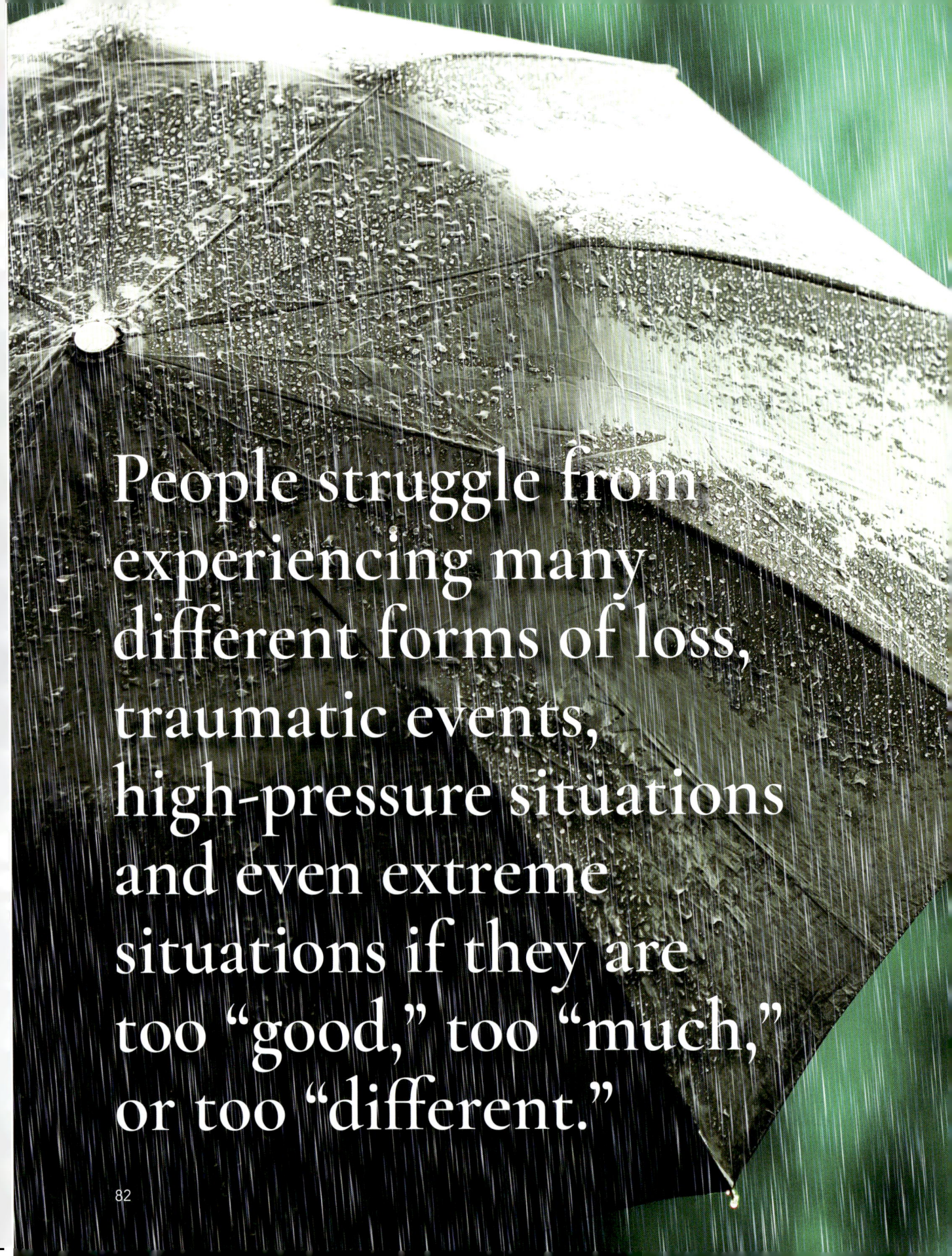

People struggle from experiencing many different forms of loss, traumatic events, high-pressure situations and even extreme situations if they are too "good," too "much," or too "different."

THE NEED FOR COMFORT IS ALL AROUND US

Death
Loved one
Spouse
Parent
Child
Pet
Miscarriage/Stillbirth

Financial and Daily Needs
Money burdens and pressures
Job/Career
Bankruptcy

Physical Health
Hospitalization
Terminal Illness
Injury
Severe Injury/loss of mobilization
Homebound/Institutionalized
Special needs—person/parents/loved ones
Loss of function—hearing, seeing, ambulatory
Bed Ridden Pregnancies

Mental Health
Anxiety
Depression
Self-Harm
Obsessive-compulsive disorder
Addictions
Mood disorders
Eating disorders

Destruction of Property
Natural Disasters—Hurricane/Tornado/Flood/Earthquake
House/Car/Business Fire

Dissolution of purpose/work/dreams
Loss of job
Failed business proposal/plan
Unemployed
Job in crisis (downsizing, failed business)

Relationship Crisis
Severe conflict with others
Divorce/infidelity/breakup
Rebellious Teen and Adult children
Parenting Crisis
Family member in prison
Unwanted Pregnancy
Families separated due to work

Caregiving
Children with disabilities
Parents with memory loss or illness
Terminally ill family member
Spouse with severe illness
Children with illness or addictions

Lifestyle Changes
Caregiving roles
Religion
Gender
Sexuality
Living Location

Empty Nesters
Moving
Adoption
Foster

Extreme Concerns
Legal action
Financial pressures
Medical Tests
Impending layoffs
Rumors
Homelessness

Those Who Endure Hardship Serving Others
Doctors
Nurses
Clergy
Hospice Staff
Social Workers
Mental health professionals
Teachers
First Responders/Crisis and Disaster Response
Fire
Police
Veterans and Families

Trauma Conditions
Crisis Recovery
PTSD

Extreme Hopelessness
Bullying
Extreme Stress
Discouragement/Loss of Hope/Sadness/Rejection/Unforgiveness
Hidden Hurts

COMFORT COMING FULL CIRCLE: KIM AND ELLIE'S STORY

KIM

My two youngest children, Aidan and Ellie, were exposed to one of the worst acts of violence this country has ever seen—the Sandy Hook Elementary School tragedy. While both of them were diagnosed with PTSD, Ellie's symptoms were initially more extreme than Aidan's. That following January, Ellie did not want to go to school at all and would beg to stay home. I knew comfort dogs were waiting at school, so I would say each day, "Let's just go see the dogs, and then we will take it from there." Receiving comfort got her back to school.

As the initial support structures in our school were gradually taken away, we felt an overwhelming pressure to move on. We kept hearing that we weren't just going to be "survivors." We were going to be "thrivers." But how could we "thrive" when we were just trying to get through every day without a panic attack or breakdown of some sort?

When we joined a Project Comfort program that formed in our town, Ellie and I found that gathering with a community of like-minded girls and moms each month over soup and art allowed us to connect with others in a safe, welcoming environment and intentionally focus on someone else's need for comfort.

After all of those months of being on the receiving end of comfort, it was nice to be able to pay it forward. It was the single most important activity we participated in for a few reasons.

First, when you are comforting others, you don't have time to focus on your own pain. This lightens your burden. Second, forming friendships rooted in something so meaningful has helped Ellie and me in many areas of our lives, so much so that I recently took the steps to become a Certified Trainer with Inspiring Comfort. This allows me to continue my mission of bringing comfort to the world around me.

Ellie and I know what we experienced a decade ago will always be with us; the pain never completely goes away. Comfort will continue to pave our path forward each day and bring us the relationships within our community to carry us forward.

ELLIE

I was a first-grader almost ten years ago at Sandy Hook Elementary. I'm in high school now, and losing friends and teachers at such a young age is something I'm still learning to live with.

In the first stretch after the tragedy, being around dogs opened my heart to care. A dog would comfort me, and when a smile appeared on their face, a smile appeared on mine. It's where I first learned that comfort is a cycle.

In the years following, I've learned that comfort is a cycle with humans as well—a cycle that has brought me so much emotional strength. Being connected with others who are struggling has helped me to deepen my relationships and find emotional resilience.

I was in a really dark place recently, and I knew the way out was through helping others. My mom purchased a Project Comfort plaque kit, and I began to ask friends and family anyone could use some care.

That's when Jen told me about Delaine, a friend of hers who had recently lost her son. Her story resonated deeply with me, and I wanted her to know she wasn't alone and had a world of support behind her.

Delaine texted me when she received the plaque:

"Ellie, I cannot begin to tell you how much your amazing piece of art means to me. I wanted to cry my eyes out. You truly know and feel the pain of loss, and I could sense that with the plaque you made. I can't stop looking at the tiny gold hearts in each corner. That's what comfort is all about—tiny hearts with giant passion to comfort others. I mean this when I say this is the best gift of love I have received since my son died. You are beautiful and I don't even know you. But I can see your heart through this plaque. God loves you so much, more than we can ever know. Thank you so much for this gift. I cherish it."

That summer, my mom and I visited Delaine and Jen, and we all went to lunch together. It was amazing to see her in person and to feel the cycle of comfort work its magic on all of us.

That's what I am learning after being so close to a horrible tragedy. Through our darkest times, we need each other and when we help each other, we feel better. Every time.

"Sometimes the bravest and most important thing you can do is just show up."

—B. Brown

PART THREE

Showing Up

Changing Our Perspective

Cycle of Support

The Full Body of Comfort

Heart, Ears, Eyes, Hands

Feet, and Soul play a part.

Applying the Skill

THINKING DIFFERENTLY
THE NEED FOR COMFORT NEVER ENDS

"When a person experiences a disruption in her life, you are needed. If you or other friends aren't available, the only person she has to talk with for guidance, support, and direction is herself."
—H. NORMAN WRIGHT

I remember when I was in seventh grade, and I was invited to be a guest in a concert band for a special performance. I went to a different school, so I didn't know anyone in the band. I practiced and practiced and practiced, picked out my best outfit to wear, and tried my best not to feel awkward as I took to the stage with people I didn't know. Before the concert started, the conductor asked the entire band to stand up, and one by one each participant was given a recognition certificate for their achievement. Because I was from a different school, my name was left off the list. So I was left standing alone after all the certificates were handed out, and the conductor moved on with getting the concert underway. I slowly sat down, knowing every single eye in that auditorium was wondering why I was left standing alone and didn't get recognized. It's always stayed with me.

I have listened to hundreds of people talk about losses, crisis, and trauma—many from years and years ago. And as I listened, I was left wondering, "If I can still recall with vivid detail that silly band concert from over forty years ago, imagine how vivid and traumatic the memories are of those who have faced unimaginable loss and tragedy, regardless of how many years ago it was." If we can remember our most embarrassing moments in life and recall them with exceptional clarity, why would we expect anyone to forget the pain of tremendous loss, crisis, or trauma any faster?

All the major events that happen in our lives change us. It's just the way life works. Life never goes back to its old course. The map changes. So then, it's important that we honor these major life events and acknowledge them so we can learn to see the new person emerging instead of ignoring the change. We are there to chart a new course with each other.

I'm suggesting we flip our lenses and change our perspective. Diving into someone's pain with them will help them and help you. You will have a deeper bond and a more trusting relationship because you cared and pushed through the awkward.

This doesn't have to be hard. We can learn that life will blend together the past, present, and future. Each and every part of our lives makes us who we are.

So, let's change our perspective.

THE POWERFUL FULL BODY EXPERIENCE OF GIVING COMFORT

It's so much more about the heart than it is the brain. The second we try to "solve" the situation, we fail because people who need comfort don't want solving. They want you.

I still cringe when I think of it. It was early in my comforting days, and I was still a bit unaware of how to comfort correctly.

I was at a swim meet and a family who had recently lost a child was also there. I really didn't know them but nonetheless decided to go "comfort them." Probably not the wisest of choices at a loud swim meet with parents yelling, kids running everywhere, whistles blowing, and water splashing.

I went over to them, thinking I was very brave, and introduced myself. I told them how sorry I was. I was totally 100 percent stuck in the Awkward Zone, speaking useless platitudes. There was no breaking through the awkward this time. I knew I wasn't helping but kept digging myself in. In looking back, I wish I would have been more aware of the whole body of comfort. I could have avoided that terribly uncomfortable exchange. I missed the point entirely.

In my haste to help, I was more focused on using my mouth to speak comfort than I was at using my eyes to really see this competitive and stressful environment and the distracting situations it created. I should have asked my heart to override my brain.

FULL BODY OF COMFORT

Why are we so focused on the mouth? In this case, to use the mouth to force conversation; or other times to use words as an excuse to avoid doing anything at all because we don't know what words to say? The mouth is such a tiny part of our body. That day at the pool taught me that I needed to use my mouth differently.

I started to remember that my brain could get in the way just as much as my mouth. As I look back on all of my years of providing and observing comfort, I've realized it's all about the heart. The second I try to engage my brain and try to "solve" the situation, I fail. Because people who need comfort don't want solving. They want you and your heart. They want to be cared for and loved. And love doesn't start with the brain. It's all heart. I think about the fact that if I had gone to school to write this book, I would have been tripped up. Because I would have had to focus on my brain; on science and on data and on hypothesis and studies. And don't get me wrong, that's really important. But the seven years of using my heart has given me the perspective and shown me the way. Now I'm able to apply the science to what my heart has learned.

It takes your full body to be the best comforter you can be. We have two eyes, two ears, two hands, two feet, two arms and two legs, and **one** mouth. Use them accordingly to this proportion! It's actually comforting to take the pressure off the mouth. Right? It's what usually trips us up.

QUOTABLE COMFORT

"Your mind and ears can be taught to hear more keenly: your eyes can be taught to see more clearly. You can also learn to hear with your eyes and see with your ears."

—H. NORMAN WRIGHT

COMFORT STARTS IN THE HEART

Impactful comforting doesn't come from the brain. It comes from our heart and body. Here's how to use our own tools to help comfort others.

USE YOUR BRAIN TO REMEMBER YOUR COMFORTING SKILLS

USE YOUR FEET TO SHOW UP

USE YOUR
EARS
TO LISTEN

USE YOUR
EYES
TO SEE THEIR PAIN

USE YOUR
MOUTH
TO SMILE

IT ALL BEGINS IN THE
HEART

USE YOUR
HANDS
TO STAY CONNECTED

USE YOUR
ARMS
TO HUG

USE YOUR
HANDS
TO GIVE

The most basic and powerful way to connect to another person is to listen. Just listen. Perhaps the most important thing we ever give each other is our attention.

—Dr. Rachel Naomi Remen.

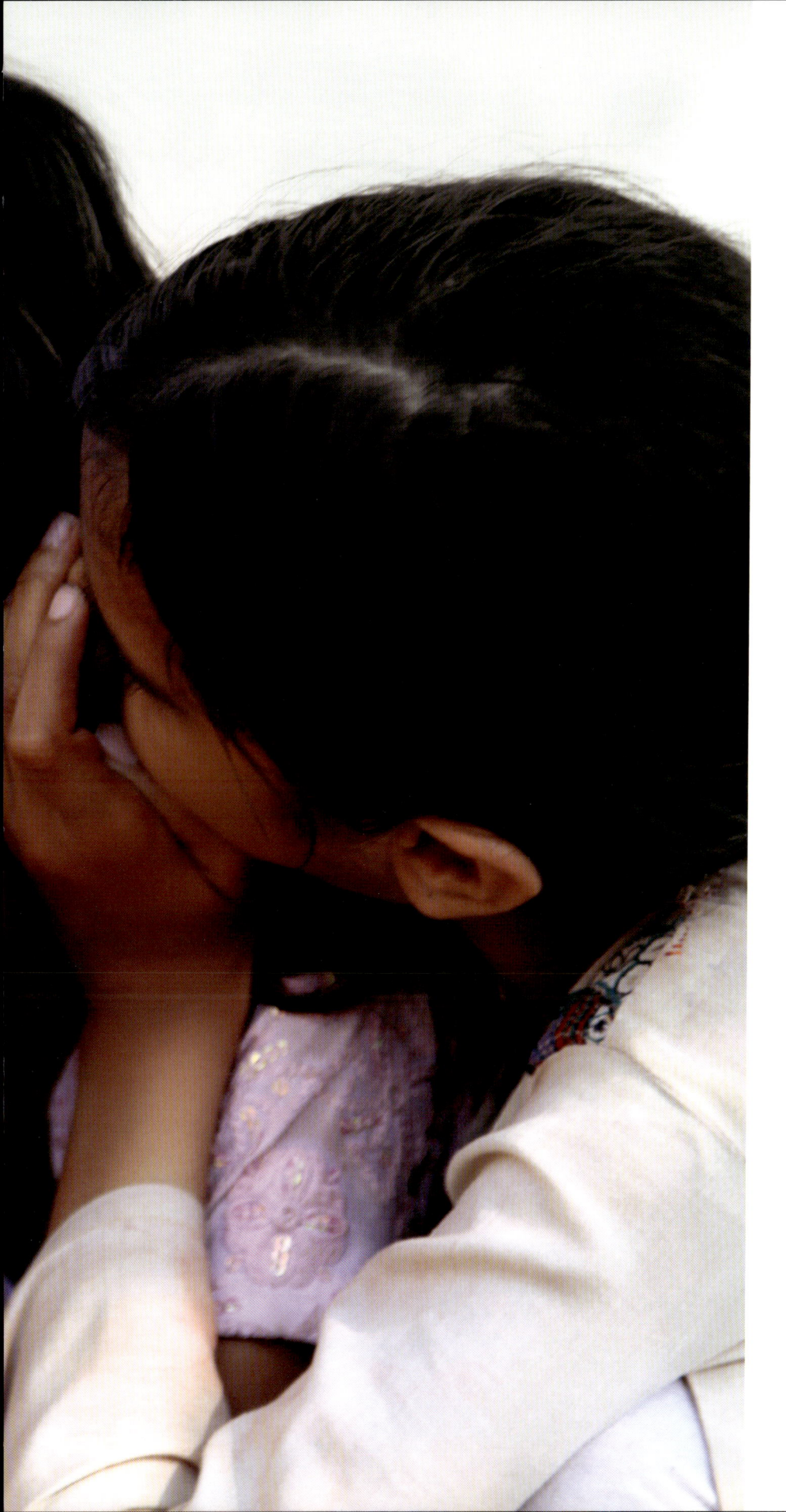

EARS

Like comfort, listening is a skill that can be learned. And like comfort, the key to the skill of listening is in the PAUSING. And something is rather calming about that thought. You don't have to constantly think about what you're going to say next. You just need to be there. In our "Comfort Lab" with thousands of one-to-one connections, we have seen this time and time again. Being present and listening are the two most important things we can offer someone.

Relax and remember this isn't about you. It's all about the person who wants you there.

Listen to understand, not to reply.

FIVE *GUIDELINES* WHEN LISTENING TO COMFORT:

1. Open your heart

Think about how you are caring for this person. Take a big breath and let your heart be prepared to connect—one heart to one heart.

2. Connect with them

Lean into them, and if appropriate, touch their hand, connect with your eyes, force yourself to keep your eyes on them. Try not to look away, even if they do.

3. Hear to understand

Look at them and really hear what they are saying. Attempt to understand what emotion or emotions they may be experiencing.

4. Allow silence

Although uncomfortable at times, silence allows for you to just be present and for the person to collect their thoughts. They can reflect on how they are feeling at that specific moment, allowing them to better assess their current emotions.

5. Listen to comfort

What are their needs?
What did you hear you could do?

"I realized John couldn't pay his rent with the medical bills piling up, but maybe I could help?"

"While listening to Sally, I realized I could pick up her kids once a week and give her time to herself."

"Hearing Judy talk about having to get home to her mother, I offered to stay late for her and complete the work project."

5 *PITFALLS* WHEN LISTENING TO COMFORT:

1. Busy

Although we recognize the pace of life is fast, comforting means at times putting aside our own busyness to pause and stop to comfort one who needs us.

2. Bad timing

When someone needs you, it might not be the most convenient time for you, but it is the time to assess how and when you can respond to them.

3. Too emotional

We are human and we cannot help feeling emotional while comforting someone. However, focusing on their needs in the moment can help.

4. Electronics

The sound of a notification on your cell phone is distracting, to say the least. Good to double-check your phone is off.

5. Trying to fix it

The second we try to give advice, we turn off our listening ears and turn to a talking mouth. Remember, you are not responsible to fix, only to comfort.

"THE MOST IMPORTANT THING IN COMMUNICATION IS HEARING WHAT ISN'T SAID."

—PETER F. DRUCKER

LISTENING BY THE NUMBERS

45%
amount of time we spend listening

85%
percentage of what we know we have learned by listening

30%
reduction in office visits by chronically ill patients after they have been listened to for fifteen to thirty minutes.

20%
how much we remember of what we hear after two to five days

75%
amount of the time we are distracted, preoccupied, or forgetful when listening

50%
how much we usually recall immediately after we listen to someone talk

> WHEN YOU TALK, YOU ARE ONLY REPEATING WHAT YOU ALREADY KNOW, BUT IF YOU LISTEN, YOU MAY LEARN SOMETHING NEW.
>
> —DALAI LAMA.

ACTIVE LISTENING

It could be that listening, really listening deeply, is the single most important thing we can do to help a friend going through a hard time. Since being seen and heard is one of our core human needs, we can actually sometimes feel our problems grow if we don't have anyone to share them with who really listens to us. Therefore, we all need to know how to be good listeners. It can be life changing, and it all starts with the right mindset.

THE LISTENING MINDSET

1. It begins with gratitude for being trusted with this conversation and a desire to help.
2. It adds on curiosity, wanting to understand who this person is and where they are coming from.
3. It shows vulnerability by engaging hearts more than brains.
4. It doesn't judge; we don't have to agree with beliefs or lifestyle choices.
5. The goal is to simply understand where this person is coming from, allowing them to feel seen, heard, and cared for.

> "The person who doesn't listen will soon be surrounded by people who have nothing to say."
> —JOHN MAXWELL

> "He who does not know how to be silent will not know how to speak."
> —Ausonius

LISTENING BEHAVIORS

Once we understand the listening mindset, we move on with understanding how our own behaviors play into our ability to be good listeners. As with any set of behaviors, some good behaviors help us grow, and other prohibiting behaviors get in our way. Which behaviors ring true to you?

Ten Awkward Zone™ Listening Behaviors:

Try to avoid these behaviors:

1. I sometimes chime in with my thoughts before they are finished with their thoughts.
2. During a period of silence, I tend to want to jump in and talk rather than wait.
3. I find myself judging them and what they are talking about.
4. I grab my phone, get impatient, or daydream while I'm listening.
5. Looking them in the eyes when they talk makes me uncomfortable.
6. I listen to their problems with the intent to help them solve the situation.
7. I like to appear that I'm listening while I think of other things.
8. I avoid talking with anyone who is struggling.
9. I will compare myself with them while they are talking to help figure them out.
10. I am very uncomfortable with silence in general.

Ten Comfort Listening Behaviors:

Make these behaviors your goal:

1. I'm good at observing body language to pick up on clues of how they may be feeling.
2. I can give my full attention and tune out distractions.
3. I validate what they said so they know I heard them.
4. When in a pause, I wait and just stay present with them.
5. I can set aside judgments and just focus on caring for them.
6. I trust them and assume the best in them.
7. I can look them in the eyes when they talk.
8. I am comfortable with silence and just being with them.
9. I remember key facts about our conversation so I can follow up with them.
10. I listen to **understand** what they are going through versus listening to solve the problem.

"You see pain with your eyes, but you help most with your ears." —*Unknown*

EYES

Dina walked into the bakery and stepped into line behind me. "Hi," she said. I turned and said, "Oh hey, Dina, how are you doing"? "I'm okay," she said as she quickly turned her eyes away from me. I noticed a sad look to her face and saw that her hair was messy and dirty, which was not like her usual perfectly straight and clean hair. She stared out the window and tapped her foot as we waited to order almost as if she forgot I was there. My eyes saw past her words as I said, "I'm going to sit here with my coffee if you'd like to join me." (I hadn't planned on doing that, but I wanted to offer her the chance to talk.) "I'd like that," she answered.

When someone is in need of comfort, we can see clues that alert us to this need. Our eyes can pick up on many subtle changes that can't be heard in words. We often do this instinctively rather than consciously. Our words communicate how we are feeling, but our nonverbal cues sometimes speak the loudest.

Dr. Albert Mehrabian is one of the leading researchers on nonverbal communication. His Elements of Personal Communication chart on page 112 demonstrates just how important our eyes are in seeing what is being communicated. Gestures, posture, facial expression, eye contact—"eye talk"— things only our eyes can pick up on. Like Dina, we can say one thing, but our body language is saying something else.

Using our eyes to recognize who needs comfort, we can accurately be more aware of other people's emotions, including how they are feeling and the unspoken messages they're sending. Additionally, we can create trust when we connect with them by sending them nonverbal signals that show we understand and care.

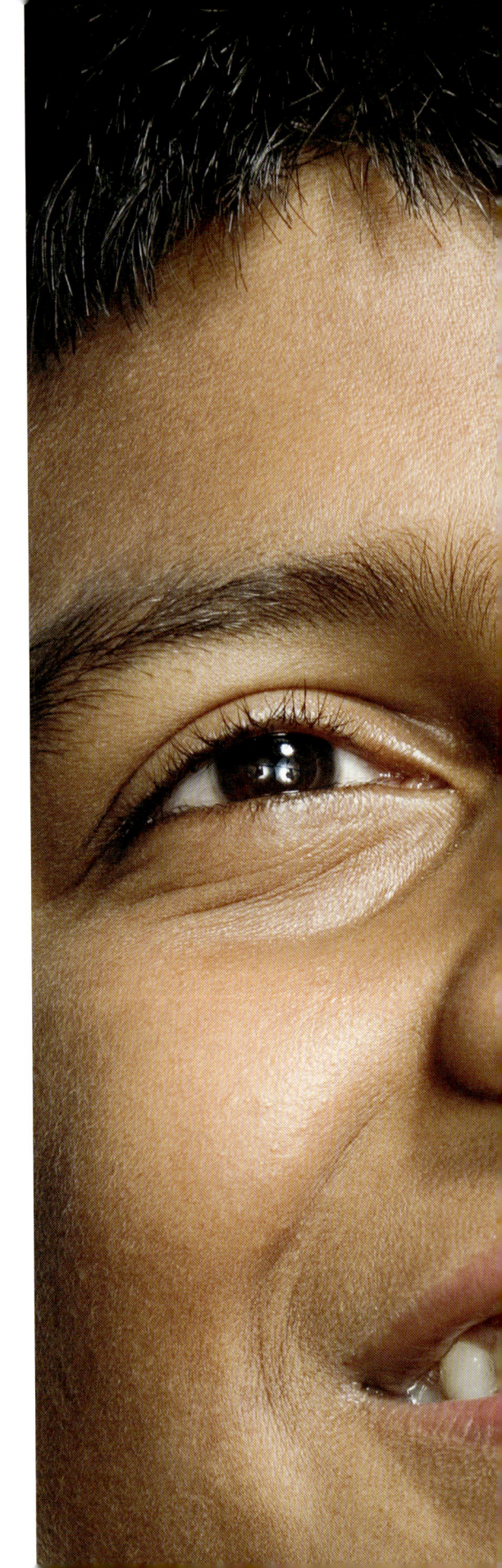

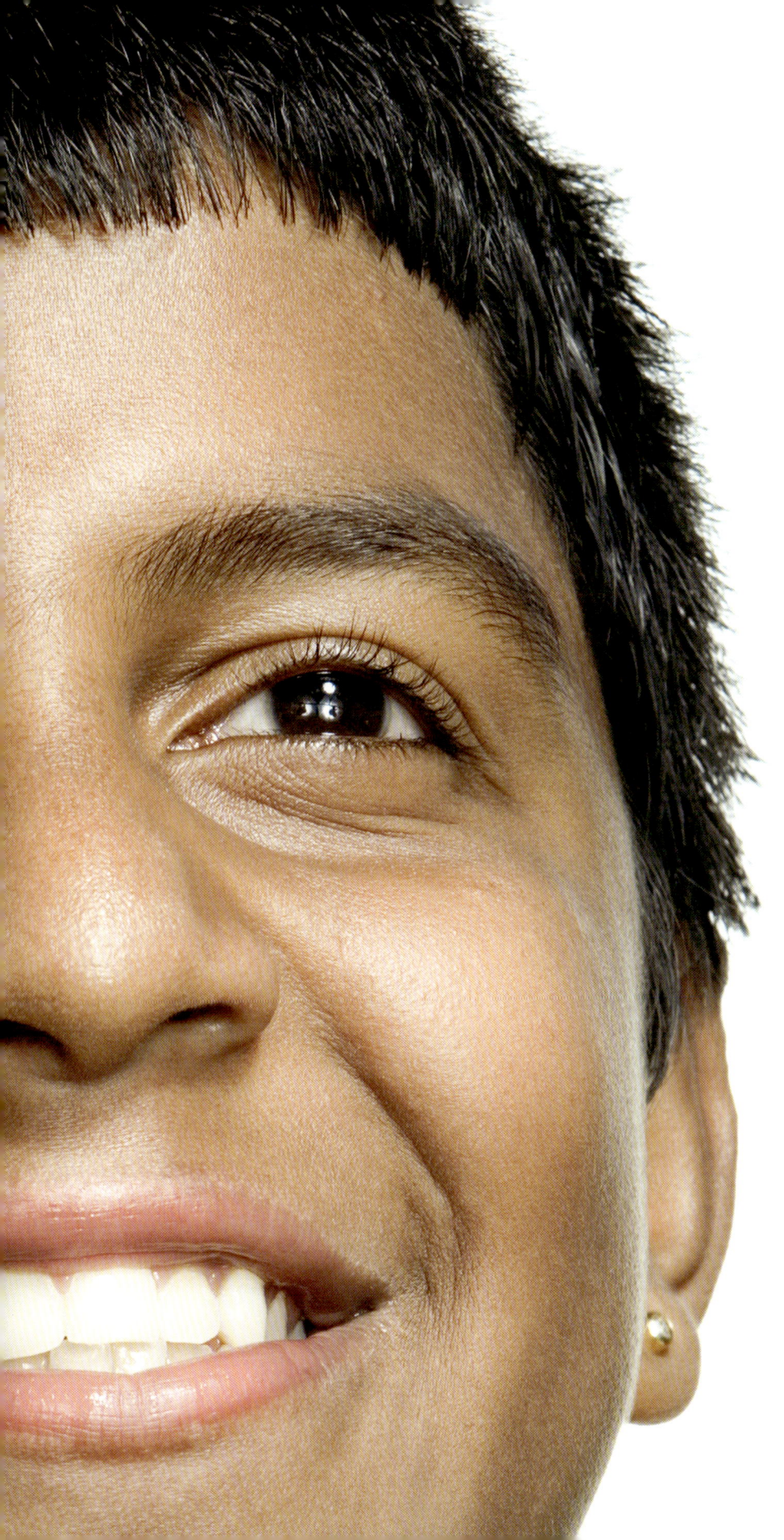

"A person who truly cares is the one who sees the pain in your eyes while everyone else believes in the smile on your face."

—UNKNOWN

OUR EYES MAY SEE A NEED BEFORE OUR EARS HEAR ONE

Herein lies one of the most logical explanations as to why the emotion versus action gap is widening in our current world: As our communication has shifted to screens, our focus has shifted away from the awareness of nonverbal cues.

Dr. Albert Mehrabian, a leading expert on communication, holds that words that we say account for only 7 percent of communication. The rest is all nonverbal. Think of that for a minute, and consider the effect this has on our current world of screens. If all we are doing is reading words on a screen, we are missing 93 percent of how we have traditionally communicated. This is a major problem we need to face.

It is critical for us to focus on all aspects of nonverbal communication—those that are not always visible on a screen—to maintain solid relationships in our lives.

DR. ALBERT MEHRABIAN'S ELEMENTS OF PERSONAL COMMUNICATION

7% spoken words
38% voice, tone
55% body language

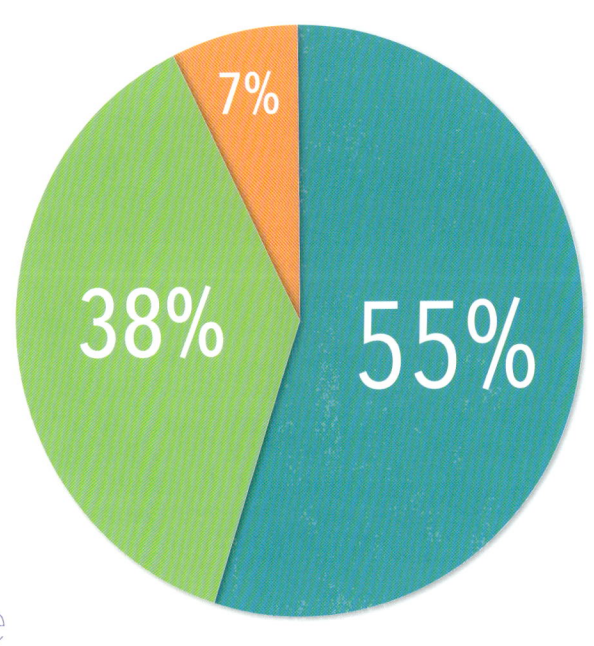

WHEN SOMEONE NEEDS SUPPORT
Begin by paying attention to these key areas:

IN CONVERSATION

- ☐ Eyes–watery, teary, darting, staring in the distance, or looking down
- ☐ Facial Expressions–unexpressive, sad, or angry
- ☐ Appearance–clothing or weight changed
- ☐ Tone and cadence–speech louder or softer, faster or slower than normal
- ☐ Body gestures–legs swinging, fingers tapping, arms flailing, or fists clenched

OUTSIDE OF CONVERSATION

- ☐ Schedule–has dramatically changed
- ☐ Diet–eating or drinking has changed
- ☐ Isolation–seek out family and friends less frequently
- ☐ Events–plans canceled or not made at all

"You need to understand that your friend—the person you're helping—is probably not quite himself. He's different. His thinking is affected. His behavior might be erratic. His emotions are probably off the scale … What can you expect from a friend who is hurting? Actually, not very much. What he experienced is abnormal, so his response is actually quite normal. Your friend is no longer functioning the way he once did and probably won't for a while. But just because your friend is this way does not mean that he can be avoided. He needs you."

–H. NORMAN WRIGHT

AS WE USE OUR EYES TO COMFORT, LOOK FOR THESE SIGNALS:

BEHAVIORS YOU CAN OBSERVE

- ☐ They've become withdrawn and don't get together or talk with you as often as they used to.
- ☐ They avoid all hobbies or things they used to enjoy.
- ☐ They experience a change in eating habits, either eating way more or way less than they used to.
- ☐ They may have difficulty doing laundry, grocery shopping, or paying bills.
- ☐ They have a sense of apathy.
- ☐ They are exhausted.
- ☐ They appear stressed or disorganized.
- ☐ They isolate and cancel plans last minute.
- ☐ They will more frequently turn down plans to do things together.
- ☐ They obsess over cleaning or other details.
- ☐ They over-plan everything.
- ☐ Their friend circle changes or disappears entirely.
- ☐ Their financial status changes.
- ☐ Their job situation changes.
- ☐ Their family dynamic/life changes.
- ☐ They display increased use of alcohol and drugs and other high-risk behaviors.
- ☐ They're not sleeping or are sleeping all the time.
- ☐ They change driving habits to avoid busy roads or congestion.

BEHAVIORS IN THE WORKPLACE OR CLASSROOM

- ☐ Simple tasks that used to be easy become extremely hard to focus on.
- ☐ They can often repeat what they've said many times or lose a train of thought and never finish the sentence.
- ☐ They have a hard time concentrating and may feel like they are in a "fog."
- ☐ They avoid being in larger groups and keep to themselves.
- ☐ They describe their day in a way that indicates they are isolating themselves: "I can get through the day if I avoid any interaction with people. I will keep my head down and avoid any situation where I have to interact with another human being."

OUTWARD PHYSICAL SYMPTOMS

- ☐ They can't relax and can be very jittery.
- ☐ They feel physical pain: "My skin hurts. My teeth hurt. My hair hurts."
- ☐ They pick at their skin or nails.
- ☐ They exhibit nervous body habits like shaking a leg or tapping a pencil.

WHEN YOU ARE WITH THEM:

- ☐ They lose their sense of humor, sense of security, or sense of self.
- ☐ They don't seem "present" when you talk to them. Their mind seems to be somewhere else.
- ☐ They have more negative emotions than normal—angry, grumpy, teary, goofy.
- ☐ They experience a rapid change of emotions (e.g., anger, sadness, despair, hope).
- ☐ They exhibit a lower sense of self-worth, self-esteem, or confidence.
- ☐ They express feeling a lessened sense of security, sense of humor, or sense of self.
- ☐ They express feeling scared and think bad things are going to happen to them.
- ☐ They make isolating statements such as: "All I want is to be left alone."
- ☐ They express feeling like no one can relate to them.
- ☐ They express that it feels like they are broken while everyone around them is whole.
- ☐ They describe feeling like the world is going five hundred miles per hour while they are standing still.
- ☐ They describe feeling helpless and alone.
- ☐ They describe a sense of desperation.

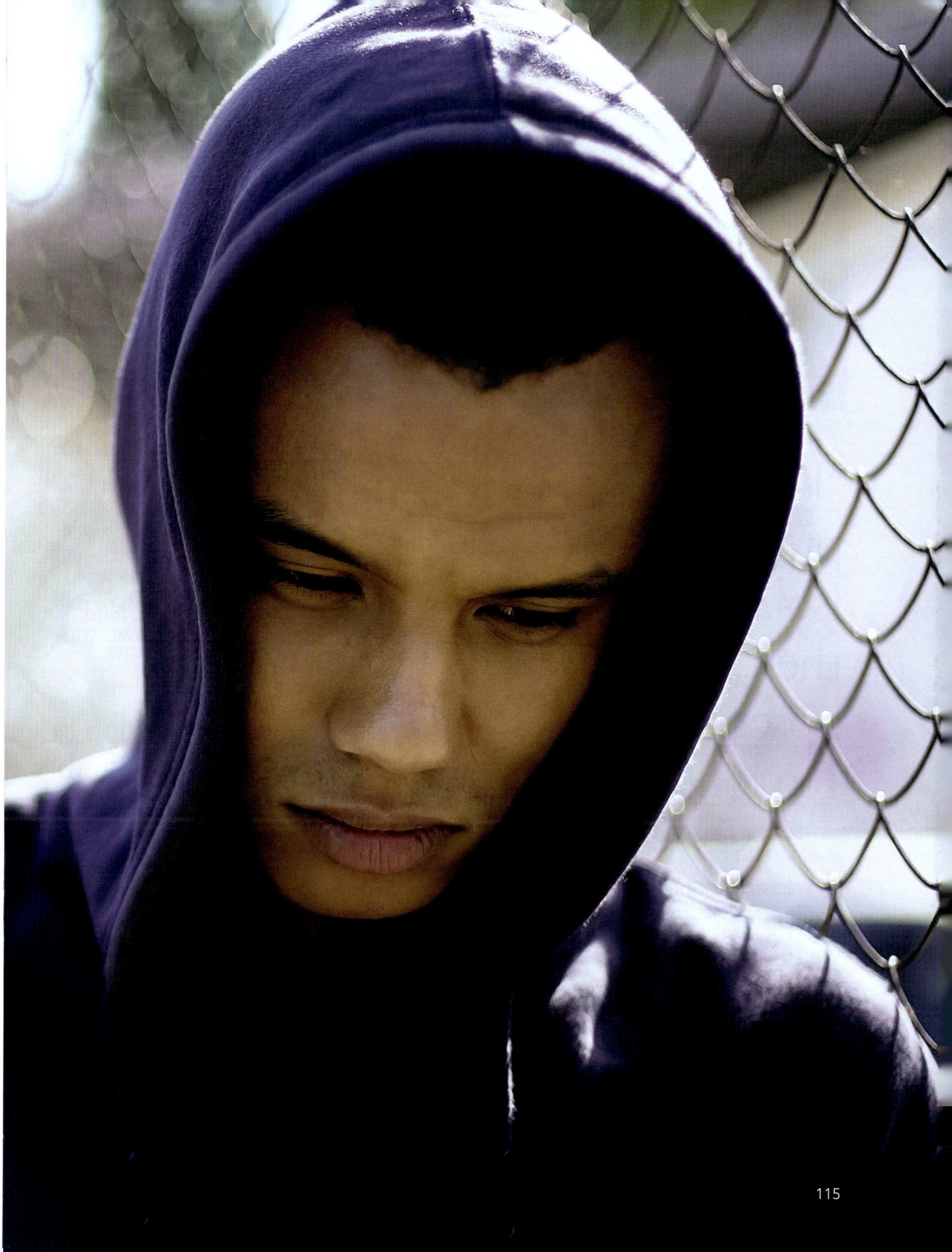

MOUTH

I recently moved to Virginia from Connecticut, where we had lived for over twelve years—the twelve main family years. You know those years—school, sports, dances, band concerts, confirmations, graduations and birthday parties. All the laughs and tears and friends and activities that had become such an integral part of my life were about to be left behind.

The thought of moving out of one house and moving into another one coupled with starting fresh with everything was exhausting. My husband had a new job, two of my girls were off to college, and my youngest daughter was starting high school. It seemed that everyone was set with their path ahead but me. Nothing was physically wrong, but my heart was broken.

My family and friends know that I love to talk. A lot. I love to laugh and hang out with friends. I am not shy, and I love people. So, it's really easy to see how some did not take me seriously when I told them how much I didn't want to move and how tough it was going to be. Or maybe they did but didn't know what to say, because we all know that happens too. And what was the line I heard the most? What was the line I wanted to scream every single time I heard it?

"You're going to be fine." Or: "You'll do great." Or: "You'll make friends in no time."

I really wanted to scream each and every time I heard these terrible horrible, no-good, very bad lines. Shake the poor friend of mine and say, "I know I'll be fine! But that's not what I want to hear." I just wanted people to say, "I know it sucks. Right? I'm so sorry. You know I'll always be here. I'm going to miss you." That's all. I just wanted people to hug me and say it was all going to be okay.

Dr. Kenneth C Haugk, in his great book, *Don't Sing Songs to a Heavy Heart* calls these kind of phrases "Pink Thinking." Pink thinking behaviors gloss over, deny, or minimize the painful reality of a suffering person. It's easy to see why we say these phrases because, face it, we all do. We say these kinds of things because we want the person to know how much we believe in them. Our initial instinct is to solve their hurt not be in their hurt with them.

Knowing how and when to use our mouths will make these situations way easier.

> Sometimes no words are the best words of all. Silence can never be misquoted

To comfort, one must be comfortable being uncomfortable.

THE MOUTH

*Be silent, and when you do speak,
let it be with your heart and not your head.*

SIX THINGS TO CONSIDER BEFORE YOU SPEAK

1. Remove Distractions
Don't let your phone, your work, or your surroundings interfere with your conversation.

2. Lead with your heart
To touch another's heart, your words need to originate from your own heart. You need to simply care for this person—nothing more nothing less.

3. Are words even needed?
Sometimes there are no words. Don't force them. Just be there.

4. Consider an action instead of words
Sometimes people who are hurting prefer not to talk but desperately want to know that you care.

5. Respect the silent pauses
Allow time for each of you to formulate the right words. Watch the nonverbal cues in those silences to guide you and don't break the silence just because it's uncomfortable.

6. Stick with it!
Relationships grow very deep when we don't give up on each other. We work through the peaks and valleys together. We support each other in the good times and bad even though it's awkward and hard.

Do Your Words & Actions Pass the PAUSE FILTER Test?

Before you say anything to someone needing support, please test your potential words and actions.

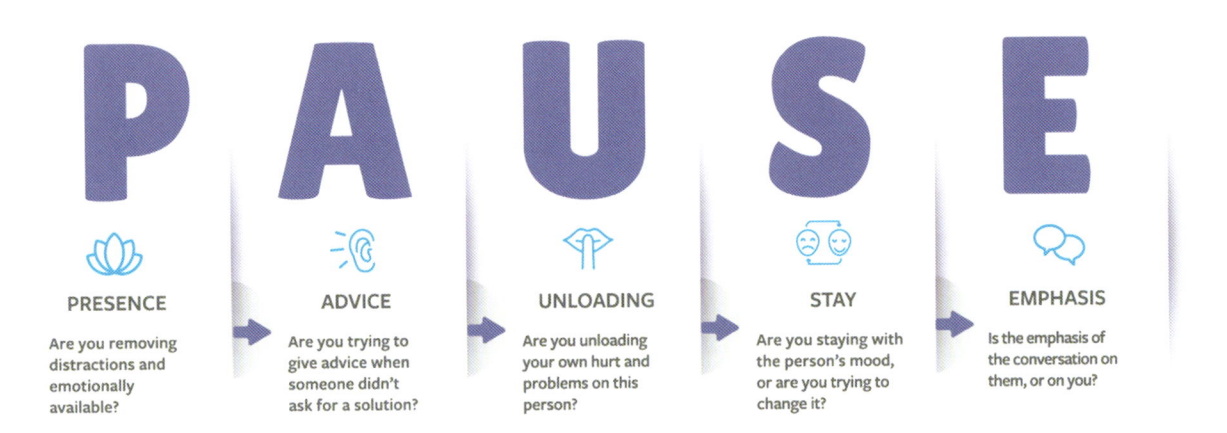

P A U S E

PRESENCE
Are you removing distractions and emotionally available?

ADVICE
Are you trying to give advice when someone didn't ask for a solution?

UNLOADING
Are you unloading your own hurt and problems on this person?

STAY
Are you staying with the person's mood, or are you trying to change it?

EMPHASIS
Is the emphasis of the conversation on them, or on you?

FOCUS GRABBING

*Speak in a way that others love to listen to you
and listen in a way that others love to speak to you.*

One of the fastest ways you can sabotage a good, caring response is when you don't pay attention to this very critical blunder. It happens when we move the focus of conversation away from the one needing support and on to ourselves.

We all do it. It happens sometimes without us even knowing it because it's human nature to talk about ourselves.

These examples show how the focus grabbing versus care response works. When we keep the conversation off of us and focus on the person we are supporting, it's amazing how much insight we will gain and how much easier it will be to show care and support.

A FEW EXAMPLES OF FOCUS GRABBING

EXAMPLE #1

John: I'm feeling really overwhelmed.
Mary: I know. I'm so busy too!
(Focus Grab)

John: I'm feeling really overwhelmed.
Mary: Tell me what's going on?
(Care Response)

Can you see the opportunities missed?
Please don't be a focus grabber.

EXAMPLE #2

John: I didn't get any sleep. My mom's Alzheimer's is getting worse.
Mary: I'm sorry. My neighbor's mom has Alzheimer's too. *(Focus Grab)*

John: I didn't get any sleep. My mom's Alzheimer's is getting worse.
Mary: You must be so tired. Would you like to talk about it?
(Care Response)

"I HAVE NO IDEA WHAT TO SAY"

No one escapes the dreaded awkwardness of not knowing what to say. Awkwardness doesn't discriminate. It doesn't matter if you are an introvert or an extrovert, rich or poor, happy or sad, Black or White, young or old. But it really doesn't have to be this way.

Take a deep breath, pause, and let's tackle this awkwardness with words!

A good friend of mine lost her dad some years back. I found her sitting alone outside our workplace, just staring at the horizon. She was absolutely distraught, and I didn't know what to say to her. It's so easy to say the wrong thing to someone who is grieving and vulnerable.

So I started talking about how I grew up without a father. I told her my dad had drowned in a submarine when I was only nine months old, and I'd always mourned his loss even though I'd never known him. I wanted her to realize that she wasn't alone, that I'd been through something similar, and I could understand how she felt.

But after I related this story, my friend snapped, "Okay, Celeste, you win. You never had a dad, and I at least got to spend thirty years with mine. You had it worse. I guess I shouldn't be so upset that my dad just died."

I was stunned and mortified. "No, no, no," I said. "That's not what I'm saying at all. I just meant I know how you feel."

And she answered, "No, Celeste, you don't. You have no idea how I feel."

She walked away, and I stood there feeling like a jerk. I had wanted to comfort her, and instead, I'd made her feel worse. When she began to share her raw emotions, I felt uncomfortable, so I defaulted to a subject with which I was comfortable—me. She wanted to talk about her father, to tell me about the kind of man he was. She wanted to share her cherished memories. Instead, I asked her to listen to my story.

Celeste Headlee, TED Guest Author

I didn't usually seek comfort from others but have started to realize how critical it is for my well-being. It had been a rough year for me. We were having our annual extended family summer crab boil, and my eighteen-year-old son would not be there this year for the first time. He was in a full-time treatment program for some mental health issues, which everyone was aware of. My sister-in-law called to discuss the party, and I have to say, I was shocked and saddened as she complained to me about everything under the sun regarding her own children. A full thirty minutes into our conversation she never once asked how I was doing. How I felt about having one of my kids absent from the annual event. She just dumped on me and went on and on about her kids, completely insensitive to what I was going through and how this party might be difficult for me. Her negative energy and lack of concern drained me. If only she had slowed down to think, she may have had time to actually say, "I know this will be difficult for you. Is there anything I can do?" I really didn't need much at that moment—just a little recognition of the situation.

I invited a friend, a mom who lost her young daughter to suicide, to a pool party, and while we visited and her son swam, she told me that everyone else treated her differently now and was afraid to talk to her. I just followed her lead, and we talked about makeup, fashion, kids, school. When we parted, I hugged her tightly, and she said, "Keep inviting us?"

My husband was transferred to a hospital in Newark in the middle of the night in kidney and liver failure, and I was overwhelmed. At 6 a.m. I headed to the cafeteria to get coffee and was looking for one of those cardboard carriers. As I was aimlessly wandering the cafeteria, a worker came over and asked if I was okay. I must have looked awful and confused. I made a gesture with my hand for what I was looking for. "She asked why I was there." I had barely explained my husband's situation when she touched my shoulder and said, "Don't worry, sista. We may be in da hood, but we good," and lifted her shirt to show two different scars. She explained that she had a liver and kidney transplant and this was the best place to be! At that moment it was exactly what I needed to comfort me and help ease my mind. She "saw" me and knew what I needed at the time. I think we need to "see" people and understand the smallest gesture can make a difference.

WORDS TO AVOID— THEY *CAN* BE HURTFUL

Here's the thing about this list. You will find some phrases in here that when said the right way and at the right time, are totally fine.

What's important to remember is this. Every one of these phrases when said at the wrong time or in the wrong way will not be comforting to the one you are trying to support.

- ☐ "Why" questions. Avoid them all.
- ☐ I know just how you feel. (You don't)
- ☐ Comparison of any kind! Please don't try to compare their situation to anything you have experienced or heard of.
- ☐ How are you? How are you doing? (when said in passing)
- ☐ Please let me know…
- ☐ Be sure to take care of yourself.
- ☐ Any advice of any kind… just don't go there.
- ☐ I'll pray for you. (when you say it just to say it)
- ☐ Just hang in there.
- ☐ Talking just to fill the silence.
- ☐ This will make you stronger.
- ☐ Be brave.
- ☐ It's all in your head.
- ☐ You brought this on yourself.
- ☐ Get control of yourself.
- ☐ Time heals everything.
- ☐ At least—don't ever, ever say at least anything
- ☐ You should, or you shouldn't… anything…
- ☐ It's for the best.
- ☐ Isn't it time to move on?
- ☐ It's God's will.
- ☐ Come on, it's not so bad.
- ☐ Someone always has it worse than you.
- ☐ You should put this all behind you.
- ☐ It was just…
- ☐ You have to be strong.
- ☐ God doesn't give you more than you can handle.
- ☐ What doesn't kill you makes you stronger.
- ☐ It must have been God's plan.
- ☐ No dwelling on the past.
- ☐ When are you going to get over this?
- ☐ You need to take better care of yourself.
- ☐ All of that is in the past now.
- ☐ I think you're in denial.
- ☐ You should be getting back to normal now.
- ☐ This is what you need to do…
- ☐ I don't understand why you are still sad after all this time. Life needs to go on.

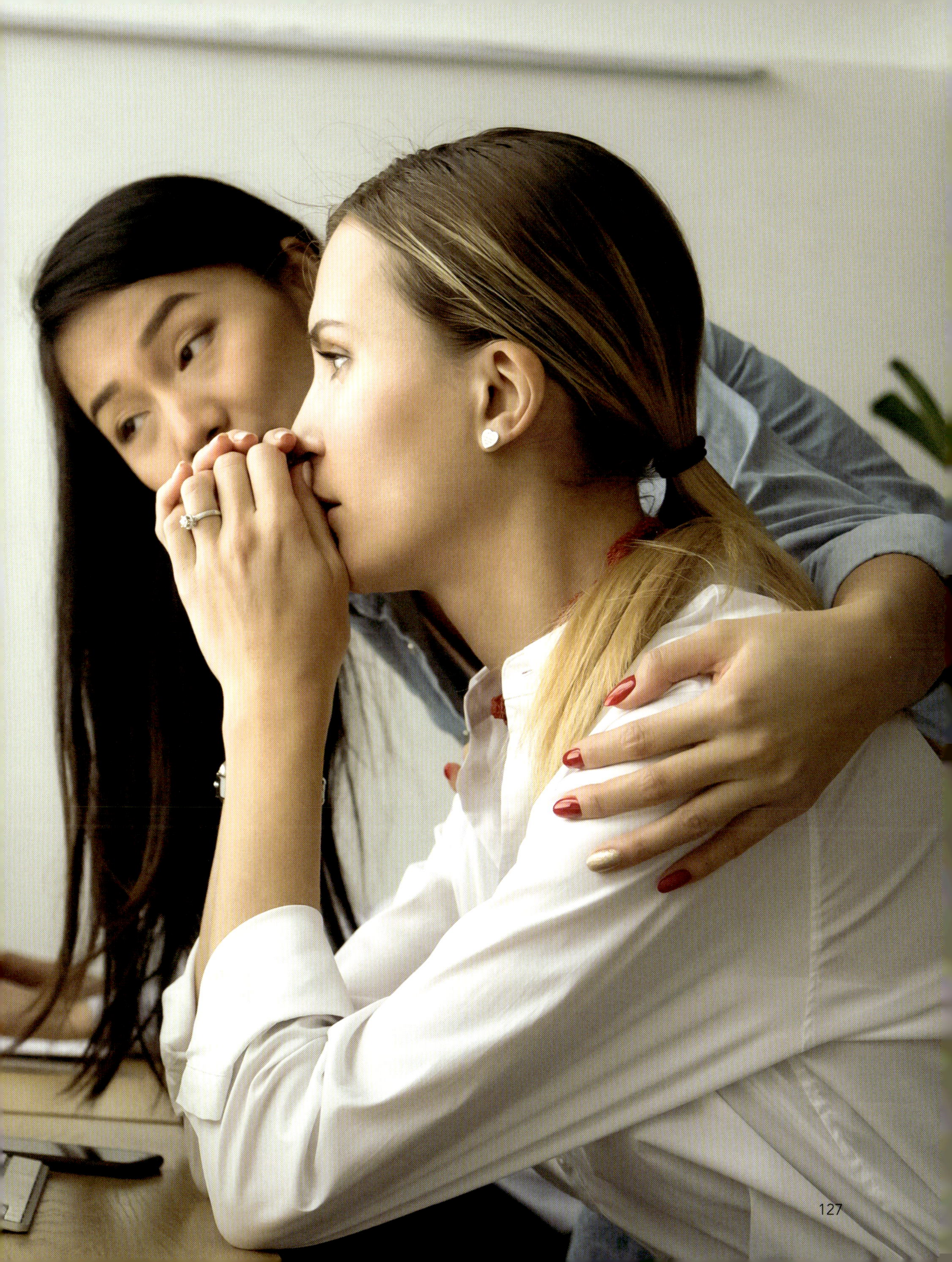

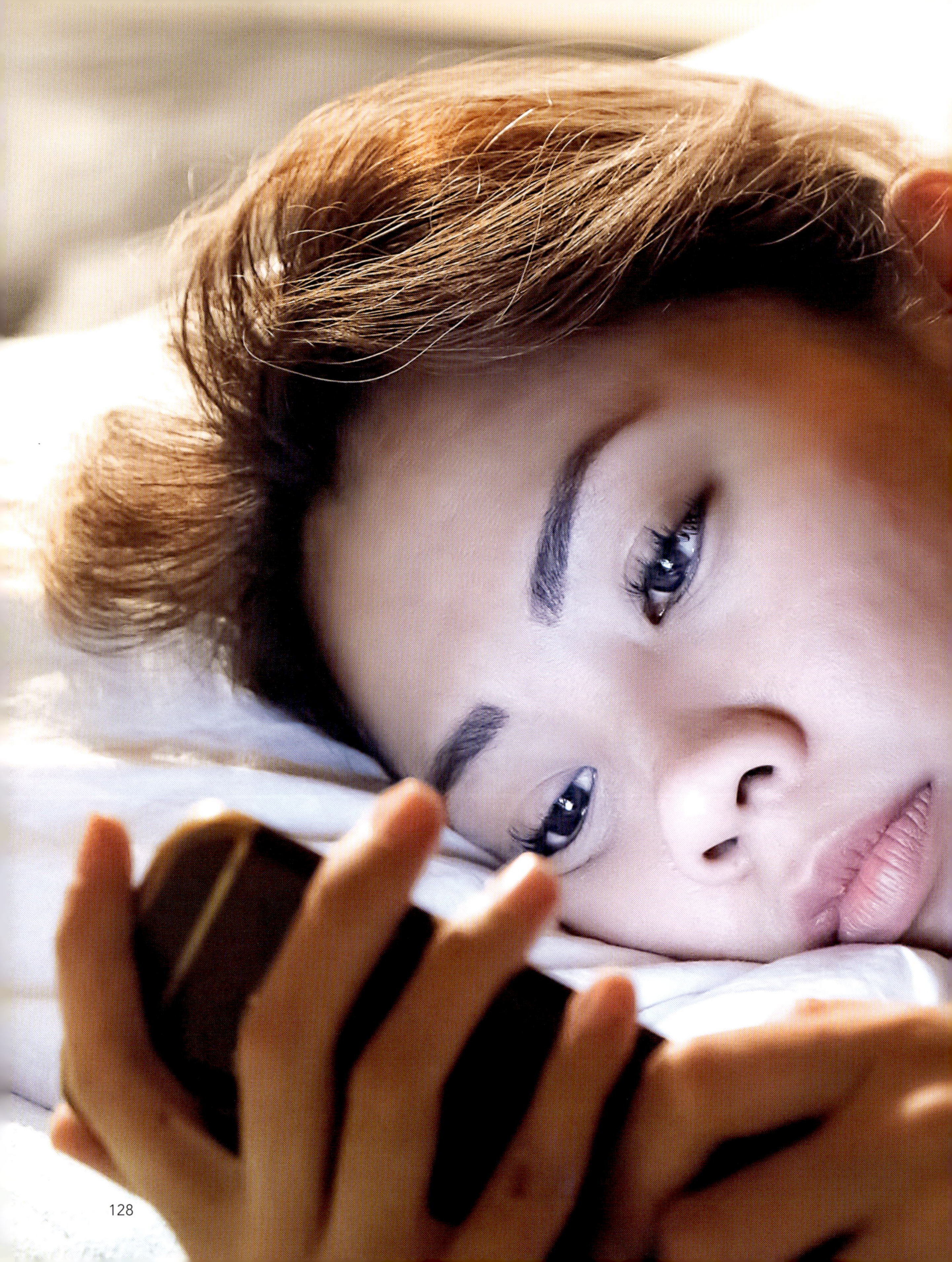

WORDS THAT *UNCOMFORT ME*

There is a time and place for motivating me and encouraging me on. But when I am down and struggling, please don't try to tell me to look on the bright side and how strong I am!

- ☐ You're going to get through this! You're so strong.
- ☐ You'll be fine!
- ☐ You'll do great!
- ☐ You'll be back on your feet in no time.
- ☐ Don't worry. You'll be better soon!
- ☐ Look on the bright side…
- ☐ You're so outgoing. You'll make lots of new friends to fill the void.
- ☐ You'll get over this in no time.
- ☐ I know that whatever happens, you'll do fine. I have faith in you!
- ☐ You can start a whole new life now!
- ☐ It's a beautiful day outside. Put a smile on your face and get out and face the world.
- ☐ You can be just like Olivia. She was back to herself in no time.
- ☐ Think of how much more time you'll have to…

DON'T UNCOMFORT ME!

WHAT *CAN* I SAY?

- ☐ Tell me more...
- ☐ How's Today?
- ☐ Help me understand...
- ☐ When you said __ it made me feel...
- ☐ I heard what you said about __
- ☐ Let me stop talking and hear your perspective.
- ☐ Substitute the word "and" when you want to say "but."
- ☐ Give a hug... actions are sometimes better than any words
- ☐ It is so good to see you. I'm so happy to see you.
- ☐ I love you. I will be here every step of the way.
- ☐ Is there anything you want to talk about today?
- ☐ I saw ___ today and thought of you. Know that I'm here.
- ☐ I wish I knew what to say.
- ☐ We'll get through this together.
- ☐ You are not alone. I am here for you and won't leave you.
- ☐ I'm so, so sorry.
- ☐ Take all the time you need.
- ☐ I remember the time we__
- ☐ Do you remember when we___?
- ☐ You've had to deal with so much.
- ☐ Do you feel like talking about it?
- ☐ It must be really hard.
- ☐ It hurts to know you are going through this.
- ☐ How has this week been so far?
- ☐ I can see the pain in your eyes.
- ☐ That's terrible.
- ☐ How awful.
- ☐ I was hoping it would be different.
- ☐ You look like you can use a hug.
- ☐ Share memories—any memories.
- ☐ This must be so hard.
- ☐ I'm thinking of you.
- ☐ You are on my heart every single day.
- ☐ Please know how much I care.
- ☐ Tell me what these past few days have been like.
- ☐ I will keep checking in on you (and mean it and do it).
- ☐ How can I pray for you?
- ☐ I have absolutely no idea how you're feeling right now, but I am here and I care.
- ☐ I'm so glad you're my friend, and I hurt when you hurt. Can we get together?
- ☐ I'll always be here for you.
- ☐ It's okay to be angry.
- ☐ It sounds like it's not a very good day. Do you want to tell me about it?
- ☐ Has anything good happened today?
- ☐ I haven't heard from you in a while. Is everything okay?
- ☐ When you want to talk, I'm here.
- ☐ What can I pray for you today?
- ☐ I've noticed you don't seem yourself lately. Is anything wrong?
- ☐ I'm just checking in on you. How is today?
- ☐ I just want you to know that I have you on my heart. It seems like you're going through a rough time. I'm here for you.
- ☐ I know you're dealing with some stuff these days. I'm here and I care.
- ☐ You've been missed at practice. Is everything okay?
- ☐ Where have you been? I miss you. Is everything all right?
- ☐ I know you're going through a lot. What do you need from me today?
- ☐ I'm worried about you. I'm here. How can I help?
- ☐ I'm not sure how to say this, but I sense something isn't right with you. Do you want to talk about anything?
- ☐ What's up? I haven't heard from you in so long.
- ☐ I hope you know how special you are to me. Can we get together soon?
- ☐ You have the best smile, and I haven't seen it in so long. What's going on?
- ☐ Whatever you are going through right now, always know you are not alone. Can we talk?
- ☐ I'm so glad you're my friend, and I hurt when you hurt. Can we get together?

131

It is never too late to send condolences. Often a letter coming much later comes at the perfect time.

—ZIG ZIGLAR

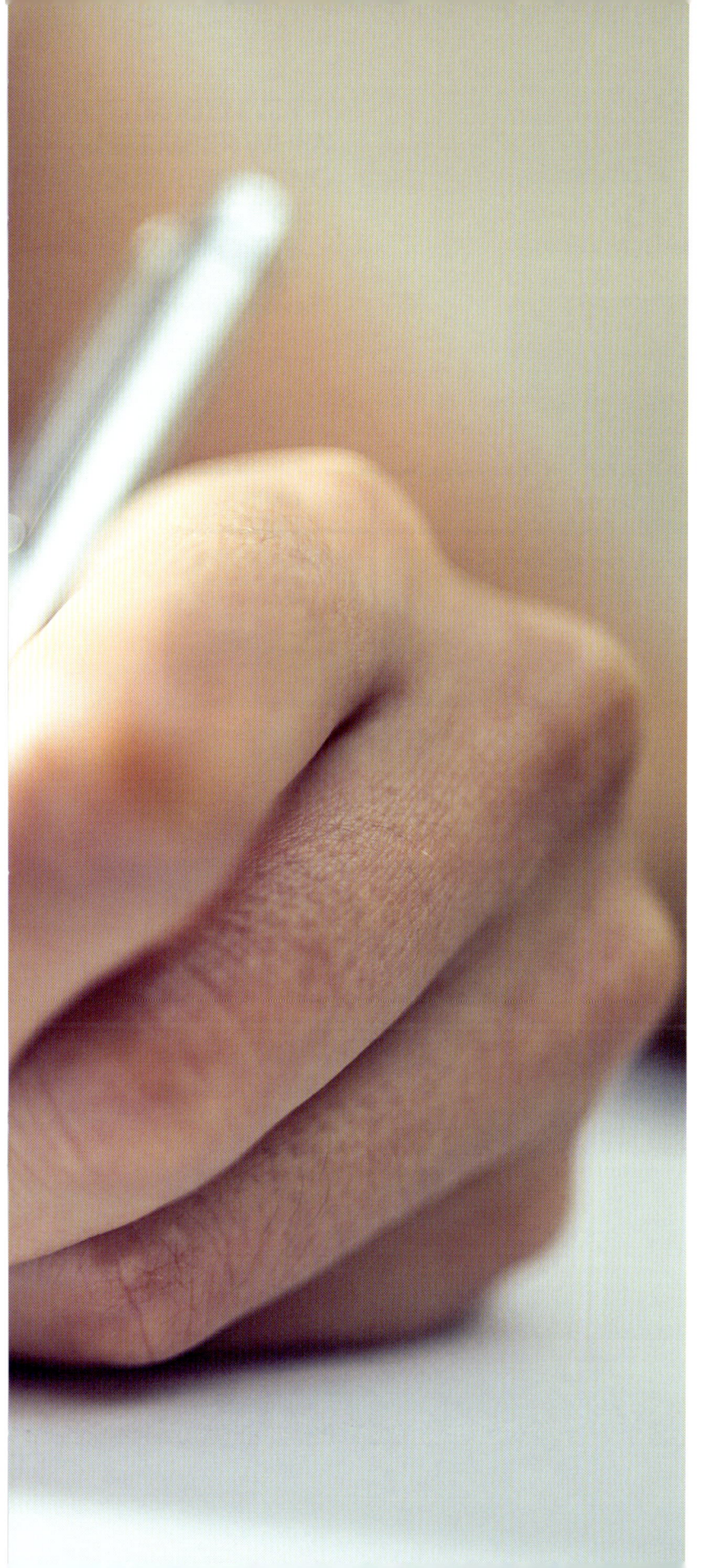

HANDS

When someone is struggling, the truth is it may take some time for them to be ready to talk. This is when written words come to the rescue. You have more time to carefully craft exactly what you want to say, and your words actually last longer. Good and kind written messages can be read and reread over and over to sustain someone who is broken and help make them feel whole again.

Messages of comfort and support over a sustained period of time also help lay a deep foundation of trust and friendship. Many little check-ins and words of hope and encouragement can make a big difference in the life of someone feeling isolated and alone.

Please don't underestimate the power of the pen or the keyboard. Written words matter. A lot.

TEXTING COMFORT

Texting can truly be one of the best and easiest ways to keep in touch with someone struggling. It's personal. One-to-one and quick. If done right, you can open someone's heart to accept more comfort, and they can immediately respond with how they are or what they might need. You can change things up depending on the day and the mood by adding humor or understanding when needed. Many little text check-ins can lay a wonderful trusting relationship with someone who needs a friend. When we think of the comfort jar and each text being a marble, it's a wonderful way to keep adding to the jar.

The power of a check-in text: "I so appreciate your text. My mother is having confusion and frightening hallucinations in the early evenings about making supper for my dad (who is no longer alive) and then angry when he doesn't come home and worrying about her kids saying, "Where are my babies?" It's common in Alzheimer's, but an added cruelty is that she eventually recognizes she was confused, so it's doubly frightening for her. I've researched some solutions (sunlamp, more early day exercise, lots of lights in the evening, so no shadows) and it helped this weekend! Thank you for checking in. It helps my burden."
—L.R.

FIVE REASONS WHY TEXTING IS A GREAT WAY TO COMFORT:

1. It's not awkward

If you are someone in need of comfort, something is really special about a kind, warm, funny or comforting text from a friend. It pops up and requires nothing but can grow into a beautiful conversation.

2. There are options

Don't feel like writing something? Send a Bitmoji or beautiful image. Link to a favorite song or find the perfect GIF. You can create a weekly themed check-in like "Memory Monday" or "Thinking of you Thursday."

3. They add up

When you take the time to repeatedly check in on someone, you let them know that you haven't forgotten about them. Few people take the time to do this, but the ones who do really stand out. It builds up a sense of trust and deepens your friendship.

4. It's one-to-one

It's just you and your friend. And that means a lot.

5. You can progressively go deeper

You can ask questions or offer to help with a specific task and they can quickly answer. A quick text can be one of the best ways to figure out "what now?"

FIVE *PITFALLS* OF TEXTING COMFORT:

As wonderful as texting can be, we do need to be careful with what we send, how often we send it, and when we send texts. Remember these five pitfalls so you don't overwhelm the person you are trying to help.

1. Danger of "group comfort"

It's best not to comfort in a group text chain. The one needing comfort wants to hear from each person individually. You also run the risk of "piling on" with similar stories and advice.

2. Don't overdo it

It's important to make sure the person you are comforting wants to receive texts of comfort from you. Always ask if it's okay to keep checking in.

3. Watch the mood

Don't try to cheer someone up if they are down.

4. Watch the time

Be sure to know the best time when to send your texts. It's important not to wake people with notifications when they are resting.

5. Keep the focus on them, not you

Keep the focus of the texts away from your own life until they open the door of wanting to hear what's going on with you. It will progress from there. Just wait for that door to open.

POSTING OF LOSS AND TRAGEDY ON SOCIAL MEDIA

While I was in the final stages of finishing my first book, I suffered a terrible loss. My sister Julie's wonderful husband Tom passed away. I grew up with Tom. Julie met him while I was in college, and so I can barely remember a time when Tom wasn't in my life.

My parents were with me in Virginia when we got the news, and we quickly rearranged our plans and set out to drive the five hours up to New York. Throughout the drive, I was receiving texts from friends asking how Tom was. (I had a large community of friends who were praying for him in his last weeks and would check in frequently.)

On one of our stops along the way to New York, I decided to post on Facebook so those asking me how he was would hear the news. That way and I wouldn't have to let all my texts go unanswered. So I carefully crafted a post sharing what a wonderful man Tom was and what he meant to me and really all the right things to say to share memories of someone you love.

There was only one problem. And it's a big one. It wasn't my story to tell.

We were back on the road not even ten minutes when I received a call from my sister asking if I could please take the post down. Pause and think about this situation. She had just lost her husband, hadn't fully wrapped her head around it, hadn't even given much thought as to how she was going to share the news and was now getting texts from people hearing the news from me.

I felt about as horrible as I could. Here I am writing a book on comfort and I make this very bad comfort mistake. I knew not to do this, yet I did it. For one reason—I didn't pause. I was focused on my own loss and how I wanted to remember my brother-in-law. But I failed to think of Julie first and the fact that this was not my story to tell. As a result, I added to her pain.

I quickly took down my post before any more news spread. Julie then went about making sure Tom's network of friends heard from either her or another close friend. She reached out to a group of his closest friends, asking them to help share the news to their networks. Instead of private phone calls, emails, and texts, one of the friends posted on Facebook and tagged Tom, which meant Tom's entire network of friends and family saw the post. Julie's heart broke when one of Tom's cousins commented on the post before the family was able to spread the news.

It made me realize just how easily this can happen and how much extra heartache is added to someone already grieving. In this case, my sister waited until an obituary was written and used that to share her news on social media. She used the time before that to reach those closest to Tom who deserved to hear from her or another family member or close friend. The best course of action to follow would have been to wait to see her first post and then share the news.

So please—do not be the one to rush to social media to share news that you know or hear. Allow time for the one closest to their life-changing event to process their feelings and notify the important people in their life in the right way at the right time. Follow their lead.

FIVE GUIDELINES TO REMEMBER WHEN YOU ARE POSTING NEWS OF A LIFE-CHANGING EVENT:

1. Start with the heart

Think about the event that just happened and who it is impacting. Many other hearts are involved.

2. Whose story is it to tell?

If this is not your story to tell, do not post anything. Fight the urge to be the sharer of news even if you are hurting from this event.

3. Follow the lead

Wait until the person closest to the event has shared the news publicly before you post of the event. Once the news has been shared by those most impacted, you can post.

4. When you do post

Keep the focus on positive, loving memories. Refrain from posting how this is personally impacting you, if possible. Instead, honor those who need to be honored and support those who need to be supported.

5. Go one-to-one

Follow up one-to-one with those most impacted. Check in often. Mark your calendar to check in with them again in the near future. Do not abandon them. They need you.

RESPONDING TO TRAGEDY AND LOSS POSTS ON SOCIAL MEDIA

Then, there is the other side of social media. Responding to news.

I'm pretty certain you've experienced this. You're casually scrolling through Facebook, Instagram, Snapchat (or whatever app you use) looking through posts of concerts, pets, weddings, the weather, sporting events, babies, politics, birthdays, anniversaries, recipes, funny memes, and the latest must-have gadget. You like this one, comment on that one, laugh at a few and ignore others. You're scrolling away and suddenly it's there—a post that takes your breath away. Your fingers freeze.

A friend received a terrible medical diagnosis. A sudden tragic death of someone you know. A peer's divorce, the loss of jobs, family crisis, sudden tragedy, or natural disasters. The list goes on and on.

You want to help. You want people to know you care, but nothing feels right.

TEN TIPS FOR RESPONDING TO LIFE-CHANGING EVENTS ON SOCIAL MEDIA

1. Pause

Take a breath and let this news sink in. This person is hurting, and they need you. If someone is posting about their pain, it's like a door has been opened. They would not post if they did not want to hear from you.

2. Stay

Fight the urge to keep scrolling because you don't know what to say or do.

3. Start with your heart

Stop to really see the person who created the post. Think about what they need to hear. By reading the post as if it happened to you, you can identify more easily with what they are going through. And that will help you to know what to say and do. Avoid platitudes such as "RIP" and "Everything will be okay."

4. Like, heart, sad face, or comment?

A well-thought-out and appropriate comment has the most value to someone and is the best choice. In this case, the poster will not be looking for how many likes they get or even how many sad face emojis they get. They are in need of words and love.

5. Keep it about them, not you

Don't tell them you know how they feel (you don't) or compare their situation with something you experienced. This is a time to solely focus on them and what they need to hear to lift their heart.

6. Share a memory

It's always okay to share a memory in pictures or words. Those are comments of the best kind.

7. Don't be a news spreader

This is not your story to tell. Support the person, but don't spread the news unless you are asked to do so.

8. Go private

Send a private message, text, letter, or a snail mail card. Pick up the phone and call, even if it's only to leave a message. When you reach out one-to-one instead of commenting publicly, it means more. It just does. It's only you and them, and it changes how your message is received.

9. Do more

Everything for them has changed. Their daily routine has been blown out the window. What more can you do for them? Do they need help? Do they need financial support or help with the kids? Can you help run errands for them or meet them for a cup of coffee? It's easy to assume someone else will step up and take care of what they need. But it doesn't always work that way. People are all too busy now. If it's on your heart, you are meant to help. Please do.

10. Remember them

People don't just "get over" the worst times in their lives. So, remember them and stay in touch. Don't ignore this when you see them. Write down the important dates and remind yourself to follow up again and again and again. It will mean a whole lot to them.

"When someone you know is going through loss, crisis or trauma, you cannot expect them to know what they need."

FEET

In April of 2013, I ran the Boston Marathon. Let me just say at the onset that I did not qualify to run this race. I didn't even start running until my late forties, and this was a huge stretch goal for me. I ran it as a charity runner, raising funds for a wonderful organization called buildOn, whose mission is to break the cycle of poverty, illiteracy, and low expectations through service and education.

The training for this race was a good diversion for me. It was something to focus on and look forward to as I was immersed in the human destruction left behind after a mass shooting. I dedicated mile twenty-six to my new friends at Sandy Hook Elementary, and I couldn't wait to share the adventure with them when it was over. Little did I know that I would be stopped just short of that twenty-sixth mile after two bombs went off. I would wander four more miles through the streets of Boston lost, cold and confused, searching for my family. I would be left to try and make sense of yet another tragedy.

The thing about being an ancillary survivor of a mass trauma is you think you're fine because you aren't physically injured. You survived, but you may not be okay. And you may not even realize it.

In the middle of the chaos, that one friend of mine knew just what to do when I didn't know myself. Her name is Dot. "I'll meet you at your house and stay for a day or two," she texted me. "Dot, that's really sweet, but you don't need to miss work for me. I'm fine, really," I answered. But she wouldn't take no for an answer, and when I arrived home, Dot was there. She went grocery shopping and made some meals when I didn't even realize I needed to do those things. She took my daughters wherever they needed to go. I was moving a little slow, not only because my legs were sore but because my mind was not clear. I was unable to process things logically. Dot helped me think straight and her friendship and presence were the best gifts anyone could have given me at that time.

Through all of this, I realized all we **can** do is try our best to do good. To go deeper and try harder. To focus our minds on all the good things around us instead of all of the darkness and tragedy. And to intentionally act and be there to help. Even if it's awkward.

Dot didn't forget about me after she went back home. She texted me frequently to see how I was. She called me now and then, and we got together more often than we had before this happened. She became an even closer friend to me.

The abrupt ending of the Boston Marathon actually opened a new door. The door of realization that helping others one on one is the key. Showing up again and again and again.

We can all be more like Dot.

HALF OF LIFE IS SHOWING UP

When I returned home from cancer surgery, I was showered with love and attention from family and friends. It was wonderful, a bit overwhelming, and then it was over. Within a week, the flood of attention became a trickle. If not for a few friends who stopped by for coffee or to play chess, it was as if I'd been forgotten. I now make a point of checking in on recovering or homebound people after the crowds have gone back to their daily lives. —Ed D.

When someone is going through a major change, crisis, or trauma, it is almost too much to just get up and through the day. All of the daily needs of life are nearly impossible to keep up with.

The good news? This is where friendships are made and deepened. When people feel forgotten and burdened, the smallest gesture will mean the most. Use this next section to find things you can do. Circle or check the items that resonate with you. And then do them. Again and again and again.

THINGS I CAN DO TO HELP

COMFORT ACTION TIPS

Before you set out to deliver that meal or offer to mow their lawn or pretty much take on any of the tasks listed, read through these eight tips. Our intentions are almost always really good, so let's make sure they are executed well.

EIGHT TIPS FOR COMFORT ACTIONS

- ☐ **Lead with your heart**—Sometimes when we sign up to do something for someone, we realize we are short on time and it turns into a stressful action. Try not to let that happen by always remembering how much this will mean.

- ☐ **Greeting**—Decide first if they want to be seen. Many times they do not wish to be disturbed. However, if they have agreed to see you, please greet them with a smile and a simple greeting like, "It's wonderful to see you."

- ☐ **Permission**—Always seek permission to do anything in their home, running errands, or financial assistance. Everyone views things very differently, and it's important to respect that.

- ☐ **Keep Going**—Help can take the form of small gestures or large tasks and is needed so much longer than most people realize.

- ☐ **No Expectations**—Don't expect thanks or recognition for what you are doing, and sometimes it's good to tell them that.

- ☐ **Be sensitive to their needs**—Don't be overeager and overstep what they need.

- ☐ **Timing**—Be aware of their current mindset and connect and comfort accordingly. Too much too soon is more harmful than helpful. Be mindful that well after the initial outpouring of support, there is a void. That will be a wonderful time to offer help as well.

- ☐ **Follow Up**—Always follow up to see what more you can do.

THINGS I CAN DO TO HELP

FOOD SUPPORT

"Thank you so much. This is really good. Last night I had jelly beans for dinner." —true story

When someone is going through a challenging time, struggle, crisis, or change, simply nothing is better than getting good food. Most likely this will not be a priority for them, and we all know we feel worse when we don't eat well. So help them eat well.

FIVE THINGS TO KNOW ABOUT MEAL NEEDS

1. Don't ever assume they don't need meals if they are not on an organized meal trains. One of the best ways you can touch base with someone is to text a simple "Hey, I made a huge pot of chicken noodle soup. Can I bring some over?"
2. Meal needs go on for a very long time.
3. The refrigerator and kitchen cupboards will get full of leftovers and old foods. The help of a friend to keep the fridge clean is a big blessing to those hurting.
4. Get creative and think of non-dinner needs. Dropping off breakfast or a midafternoon snack is a welcome surprise.
5. Don't forget the people at work. They may be short on funds and short on time. Why not offer to bring an extra lunch for someone in the office. Or better yet, just surprise them or anonymously drop off something you know they'd like.

USEFUL TIPS:

- ☐ Don't plan to talk with the family when you drop off the meal.
- ☐ Be on time. The family is planning their schedule around this meal.
- ☐ Follow dietary restrictions. Many people can be on special diets. Honor that. Don't send salty foods to someone on a low-salt diet. Don't send meats to a vegan. Check for allergies.
- ☐ Ask about foods that get sent a lot. Lasagna and pastas tend to be favorites that can get old fast.
- ☐ Healthy fresh meals are always extremely appreciated, but they require more preparation. Fresh fruits and vegetables. Lean meats. Make the time if you can.
- ☐ Include something light and fresh like a salad as part of the meal and some sort of treat—like a pint of ice cream.
- ☐ If there are children, consider some fun foods just for them.
- ☐ Don't drop off anything that needs to be assembled and prepared.
- ☐ Consider making a meal in their home if they would like the company.

"We went out to retrieve our meal train dinner in the cooler on our porch. When we opened the lid, we found two boxes of pasta, two jars of Ragu, a head of lettuce, and a bottle of salad dressing. This was not helpful."

TOP THINGS TO CONSIDER WHEN PARTICIPATING IN A MEAL TRAIN

If you can organize one, thank you. If you only participate in one, thank you. Both matter. You must remember some things, though. According to the popular site Meal Train, here are some guidelines:

- ☐ If there are open calendar days after your delivery, make enough for leftovers. Freezable meals are also nice.
- ☐ Don't forget the extras like drinks, condiments, and salad dressing.
- ☐ If you are having something delivered (e.g., pizza), make sure to pay and tip in advance.
- ☐ If possible, deliver your meal in a recyclable or reusable container.
- ☐ Be sure to label any items you would like returned. Include a large paper bag with your name on it that the recipient can use to store your items until you can coordinate a pickup date.
- ☐ Include clear preparation instructions, i.e., "Bake for one hour at 350 degrees."
- ☐ Consider sharing a link to your recipe in the "notes" section of your meal booking so the recipient can know the ingredients.
- ☐ As a nice added bonus, bring breakfast food for the following morning, such as muffins, bagels, and fruit salad.
- ☐ If possible, text the recipient that you are on your way. A little heads-up can go a long way.
- ☐ If you don't live nearby or can't cook, consider sending a Grubhub or Uber Eats gift card.

THINGS I CAN DO TO HELP

TAKING CARE OF THEM

Caring for another is one of the most loving things we can do. Here are some ideas that you can adapt in your own situation. Sometimes they will want to be left alone, so here are things you can do when that's the case:

- ☐ Give a personal care package filled with all of their favorite things whenever you can.
- ☐ Take note of all of what they love to eat and drink and do, and make sure they get them.
- ☐ Be there with daily encouragement, even if it's only a simple text.
- ☐ Don't ever let them think you forgot about them. Check in frequently.
- ☐ Send love whenever you can.
- ☐ Give them your favorite book of hope. Highlight sections you want to share. Write in the margins.
- ☐ Invite them out to events and meals—frequently—even if they don't want to go. They will appreciate being asked.
- ☐ Gather friends to write "pick-me-up" notes and send them each week.
- ☐ Be prepared for months or years of support.
- ☐ Don't ever assume they are "over it" and have "moved on" from a life-changing event.
- ☐ Write out the prayers you are praying for them and send them.
- ☐ Create a quiet "time-out" space in their house. Ask if okay to pull the shades, fill with lavender or candles, flowers. Have a beautiful journal or meditation books available.
- ☐ Look through the rest of this section to find specifics.

148

THINGS I CAN DO TO HELP

DOING THINGS WITH THEM

Sometimes people love simple companionship. Doing activities together is a wonderful way to show friendship. It will also help to get their minds off of things burdening them.

- ☐ Cook a meal with them
- ☐ Play a game / Do a puzzle
- ☐ Take for a mani-pedi
- ☐ Go to a movie
- ☐ Go for wine or coffee
- ☐ Go for walk or run or hike
- ☐ Buy them lunch
- ☐ Go for a nice long drive
- ☐ Take them grocery shopping and make it fun... buy some silly things for them
- ☐ Go for haircuts together
- ☐ Gather friends for a night together
- ☐ Take them to worship
- ☐ Bring over movies and popcorn— whatever the mood calls for and laugh and cry with them
- ☐ Take them for ice cream
- ☐ Go sing karaoke
- ☐ Work out at the gym with them
- ☐ Learn a craft together like stained glass or knitting
- ☐ Sign up to take a class with them (Park and Recreation, Bible Study, Workshop, Library)

"How we walk with the broken speaks louder than how we sit with the great."

THINGS I CAN DO TO HELP

HOSPITAL STAYS

When someone is experiencing an extended hospital stay, think of comfort for them as well as their hospital room (and don't forget their home needs too)

- ☐ Bring good healthy food they can eat and they like.
- ☐ Read a book with them.
- ☐ Bring them flowers. It never gets old.
- ☐ Give mani-pedis.
- ☐ Have a pre-surgery party.
- ☐ Bring new PJs and slippers.
- ☐ Be a consistent in person prayer partner.
- ☐ Bring decorations for the drabby hospital room.
- ☐ Bring a new comfy blanket.
- ☐ Bring a "party in a box" and have a little celebration.
- ☐ Lotion their feet and hands.
- ☐ Bring an iPad or large screen device and set them up with Netflix/Hulu/Favorite Shows.
- ☐ Program their favorite music and podcasts on their phone or other device.
- ☐ Arrange a therapy/comfort dog visit.
- ☐ Bring a movie to watch with them. Bring popcorn.
- ☐ Bring photo albums and other memories from home.
- ☐ Spend a few extra minutes thanking the nurses and aids.
- ☐ Ask if they need help with any insurance paperwork.

SIDE NOTE: Please consider everyone in the hospital when you visit. Many patients have no visitors, and medical staff can feel overworked and unappreciated. There is plenty of comfort to go around in our hospitals.

THINGS I CAN DO TO HELP

HOUSEHOLD SUPPORT

The daily needs don't stop when tough things happen. That's where help is truly needed:

- Clean the House:
    - Change the sheets.
    - Wash the sheets/towels.
    - Vacuum.
    - Clean the bathrooms.
    - Pick up toys.
    - Clean out the fridge.
    - Load/unload dishwasher.
    - Clean up dead flowers.
- Do the laundry.
- Be the handyman. Something always needs fixing around the house.
- Water and care for all of the house plants.
- Make meals in the home for them.
- Fill the house with good smells.
- Help organize and bring calm.
- Help Keep Traditions Alive:
    - Holidays
    - Birthdays
    - Valentine's Day
    - Celebrations
- Plug-in air fresheners/Light candles

"After my husband had a stroke, it's impossible to keep up with my house. Things keep breaking, and I don't have the money or time to take care of them. It just adds to my burden and stress."

THINGS I CAN DO TO HELP

DAILY ERRANDS AND NEEDS

Going out and getting the basic things done is challenging for those struggling and adds stress. You can help:

- ☐ Pick up/drop dry cleaning.
- ☐ Get fruit, veggies, and dairy weekly.
- ☐ Buy groceries.
- ☐ Drive to doctor appts.
- ☐ Write thank-you notes for them.
- ☐ Handle any shopping needs.
- ☐ Start the car for them when it's below freezing.
- ☐ Yard work/weeding/raking.
- ☐ Fill their gas tank.
- ☐ Bring in their mail every day.
- ☐ Help sort out junk mail.
- ☐ Wash their car.
- ☐ Bring in fresh flowers.
- ☐ Empty wastebaskets.
- ☐ Help them keep kids' doctors' appointments.
- ☐ Get dog groomed.
- ☐ Walk the dog for them.
- ☐ Pick up doggy doo in yard.
- ☐ Take Garbage in and out each week.
- ☐ Snow plowing/shoveling.

"My friend Chelsea brings me fresh produce every Sunday evening. It brings me so much joy and helps me eat healthy for the week."

THINGS I CAN DO TO HELP

GRIEF SUPPORT *FOR* THEM

"When my friends gave me a scrapbook full of pictures and stories of my dad, I was so overcome with emotion I didn't know what to say. It was the nicest thing anyone could have done for me."

- ☐ Collect and preserve memories.
  - Create a memorial Facebook page.
  - Email friends and family for memories and pictures and make an album.
  - Create something for the memorial.
  - Share a memory a week.
  - Help create photo albums and frame their favorite pictures of the deceased.
  - Have a quilt made from some favorite clothes of the deceased.
- ☐ Create a journal "Love letters to _____" to help them capture memories and moments when they come to mind… writing letters to their loved one to help ease the pain.
- ☐ Bake the favorite foods of the person who died… fill the house with those smells and play their favorite music. Eat with them and share memories if they want. Bring Kleenex.
- ☐ Make a note of the anniversaries of events and be available specifically on those days.
- ☐ Keep friends and family aware of the ongoing need to keep the memories alive and celebrate the life lost.
- ☐ Don't change anything about the way you interact with them. If they are on a text chain or email with you, keep sending them emails until they ask you to stop.
- ☐ Keep asking them what support they need around the house, with their kids, with their errands.

THINGS I CAN DO TO HELP

GRIEF SUPPORT *WITH* THEM

When someone is grieving, patience and love are the key things they will need from you:

- ☐ Just be there. And listen. And love them.
- ☐ Say the name.
- ☐ Hug them. As often as they will let you.
- ☐ Show up often and help them with the activities they have to do.
- ☐ Go for a walk whenever possible and ask to share favorite memories.
- ☐ Help sort out cards/funeral planning/guest lists/out-of-town travelers.
- ☐ Help them with the belongings of the deceased whenever they are ready. Don't rush this.
- ☐ Invite them to things you are going to. At first, they may say no, but keep asking. People love to be invited.
- ☐ Sort out the most important memories with them and preserve them.
- ☐ Arrange to share some of the items with those closest to the deceased and help them package up and deliver.
- ☐ Offer to find homes for the rest of the items and share stories of where everything went and how it's being used.

"I really do want to go places and do things. Some days I feel like I can do this, and other days I am buried under a wave of sadness. Please don't give up on me."

SOUL

We have so far addressed comfort for the mind and body. It would be impossible to write a book on comfort and leave out the soul and importance of spiritual faith. Whether through prayer or prayer services, meditation, pilgrimages, worship, or Bible study, people of faith look to spiritual guidance for support. However, if this does not resonate with you, you can skip this section.

I guess you could say there was a reason I was ready to help in the halls of Sandy Hook Elementary in 2013. My journey of comfort can actually be traced back nine years earlier, when another tragedy called me to comfort.

In the spring of 2004, I walked into church one sunny crisp day and felt the feeling I would later experience all too frequently. The feeling of the oxygen being sucked out of the building, the stillness, the darkness, the sadness, and the shock.

Beautiful sixteen-month-old Alec Nelson had been tragically killed by a freak accident. Sweet little Alec, the same age as my daughter Audrey. There were no words. Just intense pain and unbelief.

At the time, I didn't know the Nelsons all too well, but I was asked to play piano at the funeral. That simple act gave me the privilege of witnessing an extraordinary outpouring of love, faith, and support for this beautiful family. I sat there on a piano bench watching in awe as Bill Nelson, Alec's father, stood in front of a packed church with grace and peace. Talking about Alec, and his faith, and his trust that God would work things together for good. He used this darkest of times to share hope. How does one do that?

I remember like yesterday leaving that funeral and driving home. The green leaves were just starting to pop out. The sun beamed through my sunroof onto my hands on the steering wheel, and my mind completely fixated on how I could help this family. These beautiful people I hardly knew. I believe with my whole heart that God put it on my heart to help.

"He used the darkest of times as an opportunity to share hope. How does one do that?"

It wasn't only a nice thing to do. It was my job. I was given an assignment. When something is put so strongly on your heart, how can you ignore it?

I am a Christian, and I believe this is all a part of our purpose in life. It brings us joy and brings us our own comfort and strength. We have never been promised a perfect world. In fact, we are told in this world we would have trouble. But we also know that this world is not the end of our story. We are basically walking with each other through life to our final home. Picking each other up. Taking each other's hands and holding each other up when we don't have the strength to stand ourselves.

When I look back on this situation and what faith did here, I first see that faith gave Bill the peace and strength to stand up and give hope. I then see that faith put the desire on my heart to help and gave me the motivation and words to show up again and again. I watched as Bill and his beautiful wife Adriann relied on their faith to find the strength to go forward each and every day.

Comforting the Nelson family brought me comfort and grew my faith. This helping gave comfort to the Nelson family and grew their faith. And now, fifteen years and many, many moments of caring and prayer later, I have a beautiful faith-filled friendship with a family I hadn't known before this happened.

That is the Soul Circle of Comfort.

The Five Steps to Soul Comfort

These are adapted to my Christian beliefs and practices. Please feel free to adapt to your own practices:

1. Be Aware. Pray for God to grow your desire to help and to open your eyes to those needing comfort.

2. Respond to the call. When someone is put on your heart to help, know that God has prepared you in advance to do this job. You are ready and capable. No one else can do the role that is put on your heart.

3. Walk with them. Recognize that you are in this for the long haul. Comfort is not a one and done task. This person or persons needs you and your time for months and years to come.

4. Pray for them. Keep them covered in prayer. Pray for them and with them. Add them to prayer chains if they agree.

5. Give gratitude to God for being entrusted with this assignment and for growing your friendship and faith through this process.

"If you take care of your employees, they will take care of your customers, and your business will take care of itself."

—J.W. "Bill" Marriott

PART FOUR

A CULTURE OF CARE

What is a Culture of Care?

What Experts are Saying

The Cost of Not Caring

CREATING A CULTURE OF CARE

"Workplace culture, like life, is all about how you make people feel. It's that simple, and it's that hard."

My first ambition at the age of five was to become an airline stewardess. I knew from a very young age that I wanted to see the world, so by no accident, my first career was in international business development. Traveling the globe, working with incredibly diverse cultures for fifteen years, and living in London and Amsterdam for three of them was an experience I am forever grateful for. It was no accident that I married a hotel executive.

Because of these factors, I consider myself pretty astute when it comes to hospitality. If I feel cared for, I will be loyal to your airline and put your hotel on the top of my list when I return. Nothing is better than being welcomed by name with a warm smile after a long day of traveling. Conversely, a room key that doesn't work, a long line at check-in, or a room that is too hot or cold will leave me frustrated.

When my husband Dave joined me on this journey of care, we were excited to explore this intersection of comfort and hospitality—and it's big.

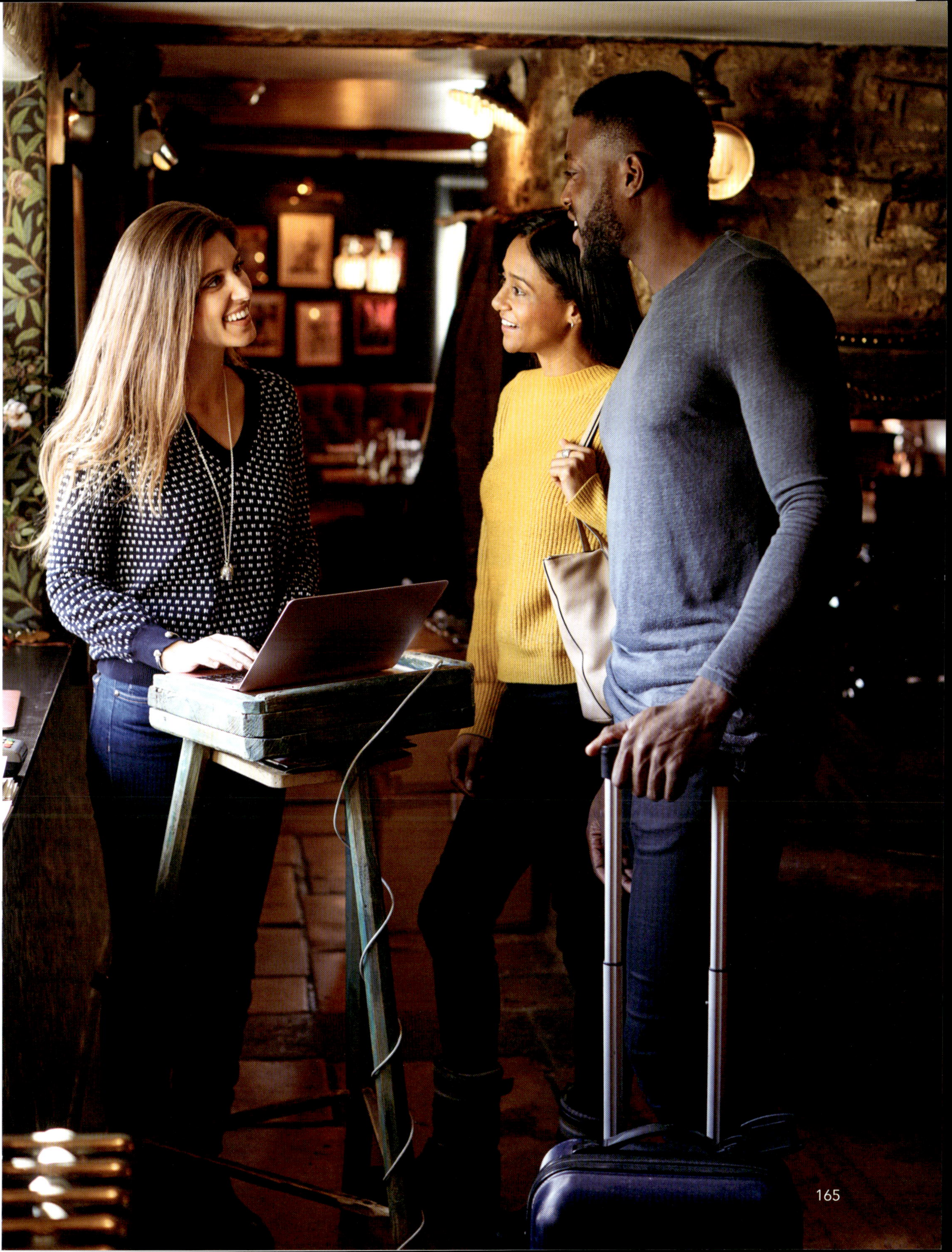

"Every single employee is someone's son or someone's daughter. Like a parent, a leader of a company is responsible for their precious lives."

—SIMON SINEK

THE COST OF NOT CARING FOR THOSE NEEDING COMFORT IN OUR WORKPLACES AND COMMUNITIES

An employee who feels unsupported, misunderstood and/or afraid to share key life events:

1. Is not as dedicated to his colleagues and manager
2. Is not as loyal to the organization
3. Is more likely to call in sick and take days off
4. Will not exceed expectations, has difficulty meeting expectations and will most likely operate in a below expectations mode due to lack of concentration and impaired decision-making.
5. May cause conflict and divisiveness because at the core of it all is the simple fact that hurting people, hurt people.
6. Gossip happens, rumors start, and discourse reigns supreme.
7. Managers will spend their time taking care of symptoms but not the root of the problem. Not able to offer solutions, only putting out fires.

It doesn't take the HR department to fix this. It's human interaction and caring and concern that is needed. And every one of us can learn how to do that better.

As we saw in our earlier stories, people need meaningful connections from coworkers and staff just as they would from other close friends and family. When these needs aren't met, there are both quantifiable and qualifiable results.

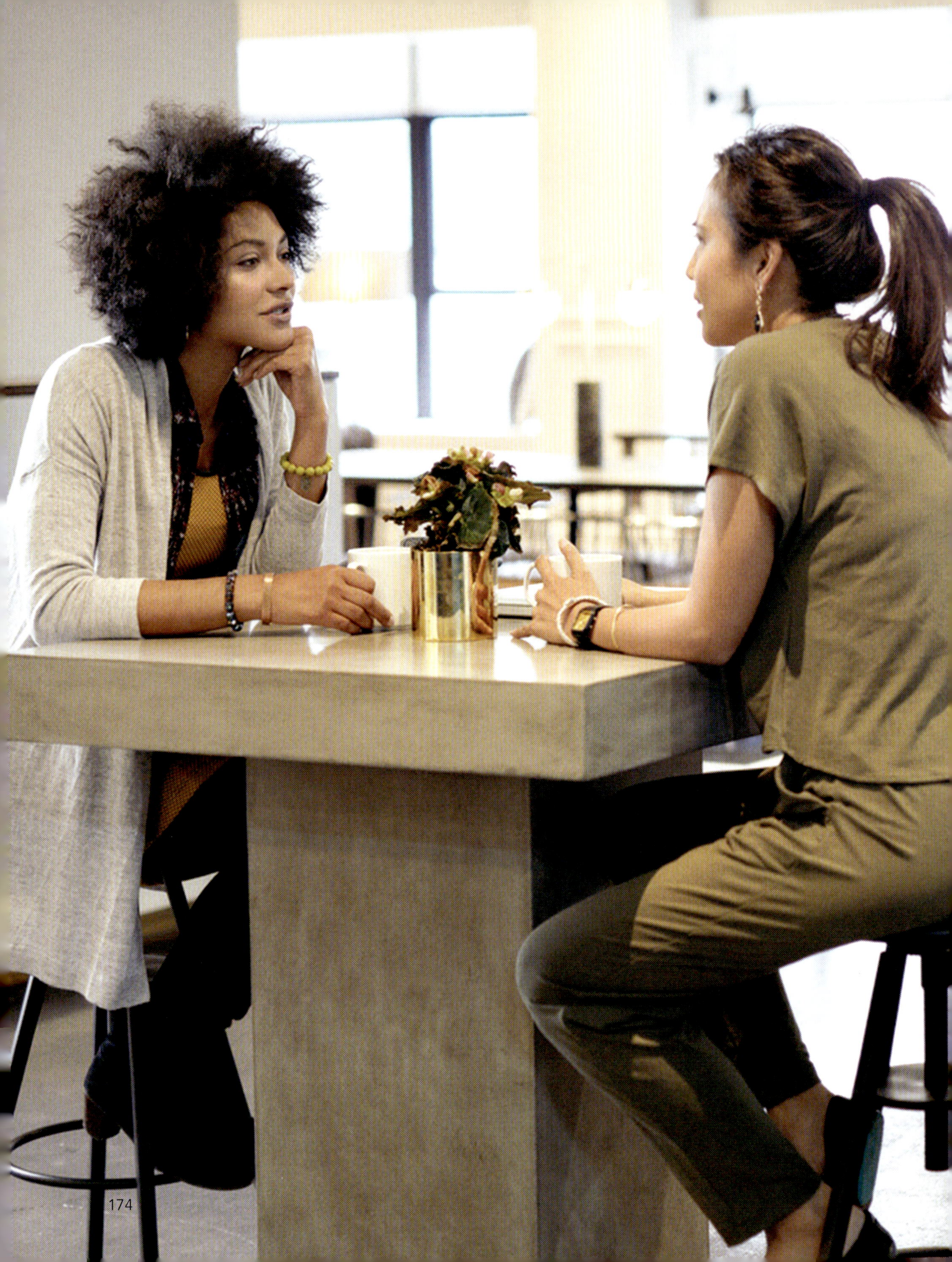

If you could only sense how important you are to the lives of those you meet; how important you can be to the people you may never even dream of. There is something of yourself that you leave at every meeting with another person.

—FRED ROGERS

"Sometimes our best teachers of humanity aren't even human."

PART FIVE

WHO SHOWS UP BEST?

The Magic of a Dog

Lessons we learn from dogs

THE MAGIC OF A DOG: BUILT TO COMFORT

Why do dogs make the perfect comfort machines? Let's start with the fact that they have the brain of a two- to three-year-old human. Emotions are too complicated for them to understand, so they are all action.

They are the perfect model for us.

FUR
Hugging a dog can reduce your levels of the stress-hormone cortisol.

TAIL
The wag-o-meter is one of the best social cues out there. Wagging tails show happiness. Between the leg tails show feelings of threat.

BRAIN
The mind of a dog is similar to the mind of a two- to 3-year-old human. They are full of curiosity, adventure, trust, and joy.

EYES
Dogs don't rely on their eyes like humans. They see only shades of yellow and blue, and their vision is best at dusk and dawn.

NOSE
A dog's sense of smell is up to one hundred thousand times more accurate than ours. Their ability to pick up human emotions is through their nose.

MOUTH
While we're busy talking, dogs "talk" with their ears, eyes, body posture, fur elevation, tail wags, and more.

EARS
Dogs' ability to distinguish who they are with is based more on hearing than sight.

HEART
Because their brain is less mature than a human's, dogs operate mostly from the heart. This explains a lot.

179

LESSONS WE LEARN FROM OUR DOGS

Some experts among us instinctively know how to comfort those who are hurting. Dogs. Watching and learning from them is a great place to start our journey of comfort. Think about how you feel when you're with your pup. And then remember. Connecting with humans around you who are struggling can be like that. It doesn't have to be hard. Be like Fido.

THEY RECOGNIZE WHEN YOU'RE HURTING

If you have a dog, you know how they pay attention. They always seem to "know" when you need them. If you're having a bad day, they are there at your side. If you're home sick they snuggle with you. They are always looking for ways to love you because that's what makes them happy. As humans, we are not as good at this. We spend most of our time thinking about our own hurts instead of others who are hurting.

THEY LISTEN

They are always just here to love you and listen. They don't talk back. They don't try to give you advice. They just listen. For many of us humans, this is very hard to do. We are busy and listening is slow. We want results fast when comfort is not at all about a quick fix. We watch our love for dogs increase when they let us vent and love us back. We can do the same for each other.

THEY DON'T JUDGE OR HOLD GRUDGES

Sometimes we have a hard time letting go of things that bother us about each other. We make assumptions and judgments, and this gets in the way of connecting. We avoid each other, get frustrated, and let bad feelings simmer. Dogs don't think this way. They just see someone they love and want to be with. They forgive. Dogs always forgive. They don't hold our mistakes against us. And this makes us love them even more.

THEY DON'T NEED WORDS

Sometimes we just don't know what to say to people when they are struggling. We are afraid to say the wrong thing and make things worse. Many times, we avoid any interaction with that person because of this fear. Then we watch dogs. And it ends up not being so much about the words but rather, the caring loving hugs, the eye-to-eye contact, and most of all just being together. Comfort does not have to be about what we say.

THEY HELP US GET OUT OF OUR OWN HEADS

In our sadness and brokenness, we can sometimes focus most of our attention on ourselves and our own problems. We overthink things. Something about a dog snaps us out of that. Because as much as they take care of us, we feel the urge to take care of them. And that pulls the focus off of us, and by helping them, we actually help ourselves.

THEY WANT TO BE WITH US

Dogs don't withdraw when life gets them down. They don't put headphones on and go through life ignoring other dogs or people. They are pack animals and so are we. They are happiest when they are around dogs or people. We are the same. We are wired to be happiest when we share life together. Our ups and downs, our hurts, and our fears. We are not at our best when we are alone.

THEY COMFORT ANYONE AND EVERYONE

They comfort those they don't know without any bit of awkwardness. Have you ever watched a dog go up to a total stranger wagging its tail? And in doing so, making that person happy? We humans don't think that way. We avoid people we don't know even if we know they are hurting. Dogs help fill the gap of loneliness for many people because of this. They love to help. We can do that too.

THEY SHOW UP

Again and again and again for as long as they live. Comfort is not a one and done kind of action. People need comfort every day. Over and over. And when we watch dogs, we see how they blend together, comforting and loving and playing. Sometimes within a span of minutes. They intuitively know what is needed at any given time. We can learn from this.

THEY ARE LOYAL

They always assume the best in us. They give us the benefit of the doubt every time. Humans are sometimes afraid to share our feelings with others. It could be that we are afraid that our friends won't keep it to themselves and will share it with others or announce it to the world on social media. Dogs don't think that way. No shaming and blaming in their world. They are loyal and confidential. And this makes us love them all the more.

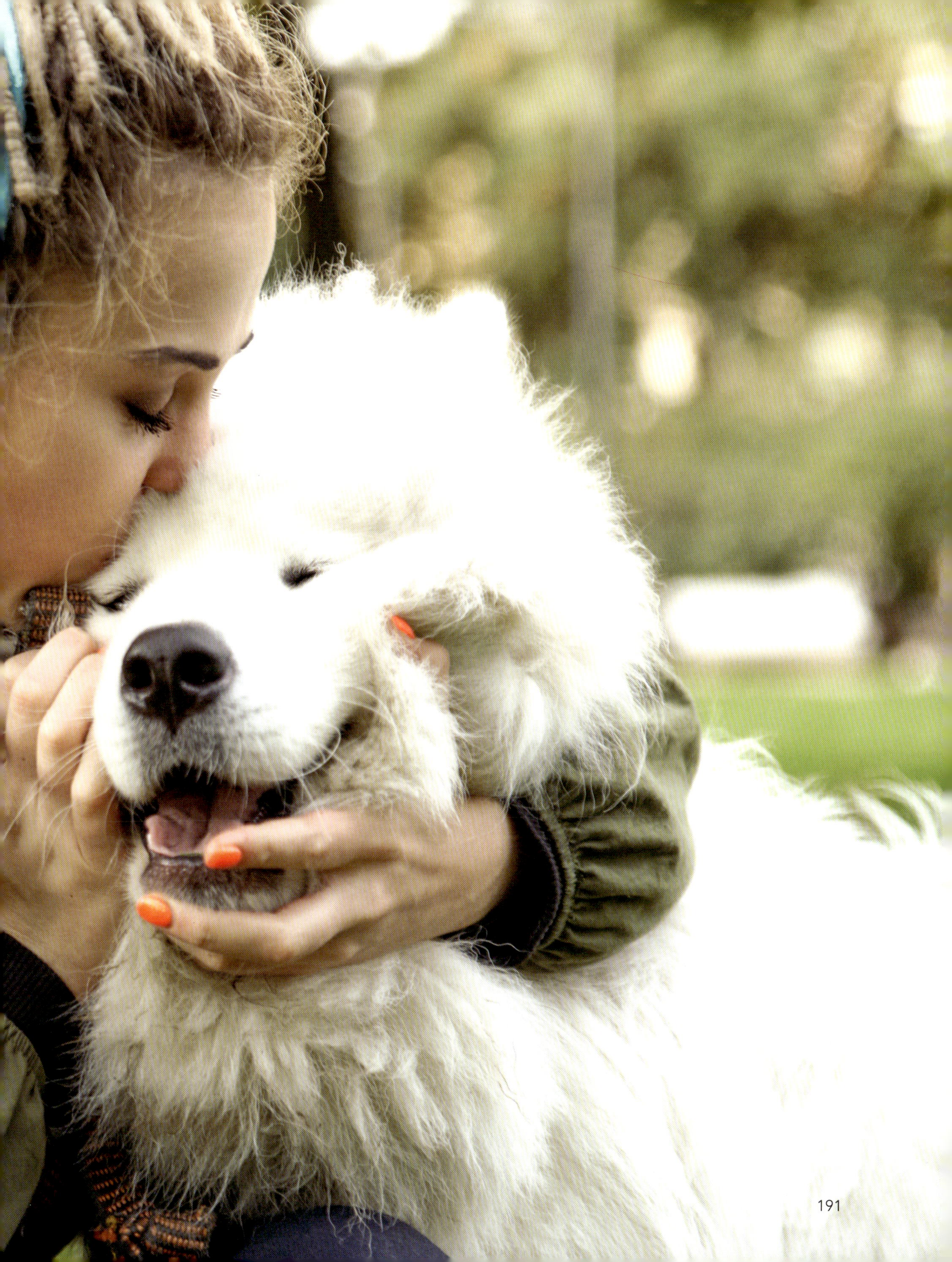

THEY BRING JOY

They don't take life too seriously. They know when to comfort, but they also know when to lighten the mood. They can do something so silly that you can't help but laugh even when you are at your lowest. And for these bits of laughter, we love them even more and love to have them around. You can bring joy too.

THEY ARE UNITERS—NOT DIVIDERS

They are inclusive, not exclusive. There is no such thing as a "clique" with dogs. They bring people together. They allow us to focus on what unites us instead of what divides us apart. They choose love first above anything else. And in today's divisive and critical society, this is something we can all learn from.

THEY ARE GENUINE

They always reflect who they are and aren't worried about what people think. They don't Photoshop images on an Instagram page. They don't hide their feelings, and they don't compare themselves with others. When they want to play, we know it. When they are hungry, we know it. And when they just want attention, we know that too. And we love them for it.

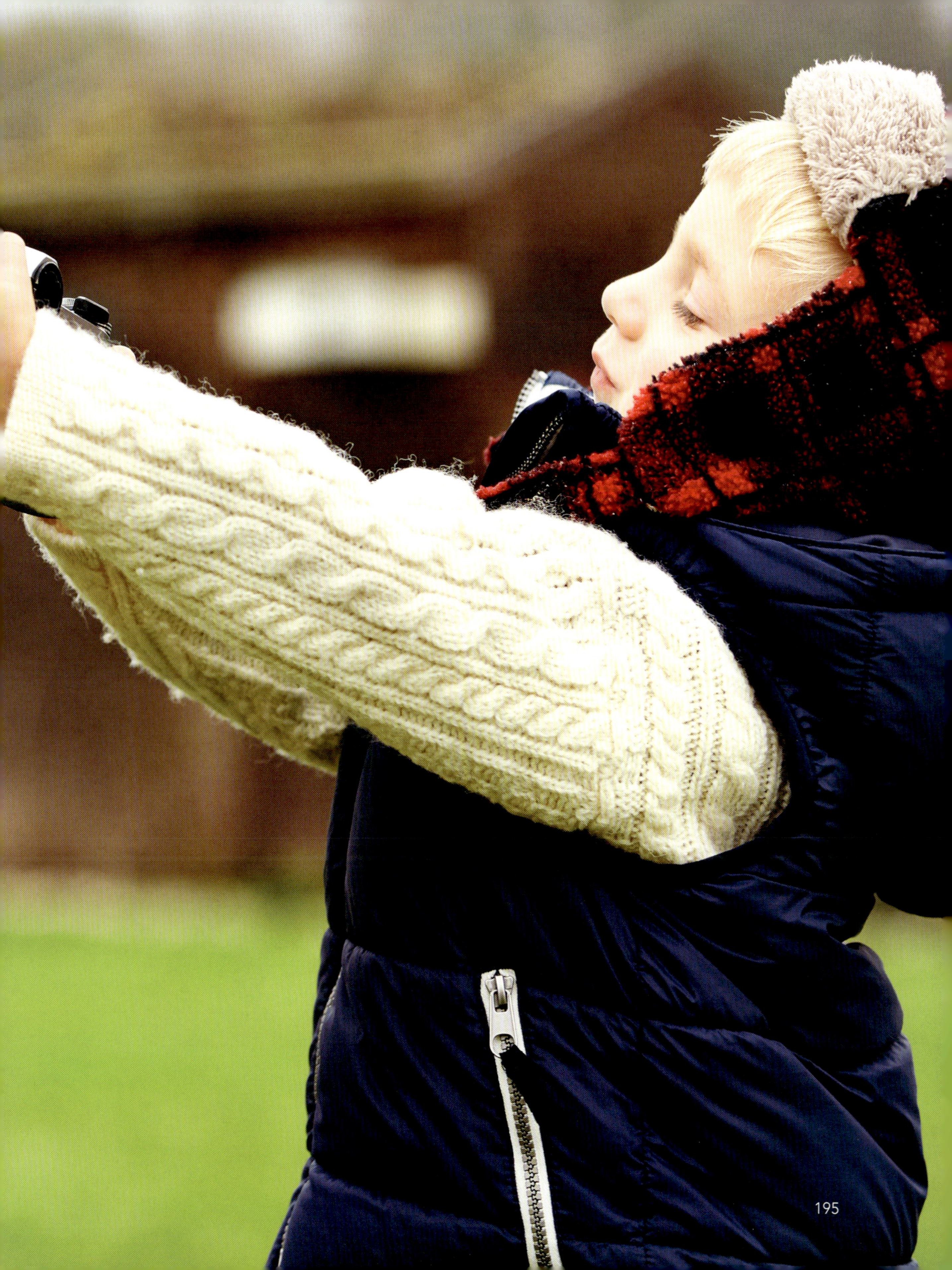

DIVERSITY NEVER GETS IN THEIR WAY

Dogs are incredibly diverse with more than four hundred breeds. And they don't let any characteristics of their breed get in their way of connecting with others and loving them. There simply is no delineation along the lines of fur color or fur length or floppy ears or pointy ears or long tails or short tails or tall or short. Go to a dog park if you want to watch this in action.

THEY PAWS

They slow down when they need to and never get too busy. They instinctively know how to manage their time and take care of their whole body so they can take care of others, "pawsing" to see, to do, to love, to play, and to rest. This is the key to comforting others, and you can do this too.

THEY PLAY

Playing is fun for sure. We have as much fun playing with our dogs as they have fun playing with us. But playing serves a more important purpose for dogs. It keeps them physically and mentally strong. We need that too.

THEY DO THIS EVERY DAY

It's who they are. It's who we should be. They will wake up and do it all again tomorrow. They spend their lives focused on others. Each moment of each day, they want to be with others and make them happy. It's their DNA. It's also in our DNA, but most of us have allowed personal fears and troubles to suppress our innate ability to comfort.

FINAL THOUGHTS

Dear Friends,

Thank you. For picking up this book and for taking intentional action to help mend our hurting world.

The pandemic and recent world events have left so many feeling broken, alone, and uncertain. We are tired and weary.

There is a need, and you can now be part of the solution. Even better, it's a solution that can add deep meaning and purpose in your own life. For it's in helping others where we make a difference. When we make a difference, we feel empowered and when we feel empowered, we feel purpose.

People who need comfort carry many difficult emotions - anxiety, hopelessness, fear, guilt, loneliness, depression, anger, envy and bitterness as a start. They can become a different version of the person you know. This can be hard to face. You don't know how to respond. It's awkward.

The best remedy is for a friend to find them and for comfort to find them.

You can be the one that finds that friend holding on by a thread, thinking no one cares. You can be the comfort that brings some light and love to someone feeling only dark.

Like my dad was to me last year. My family had suffered numerous setbacks and losses. Dreams seemed to shatter and people we loved were no longer with us. But it was when a dear friend of mine lost her son, that I felt the darkness invade my soul and truly felt that I had no more to give.

It was an email from my dad that showed me the way forward. I am a person of faith and so this message hit me in my core:

Dear dear Jen,

I remember so many times as you were growing up that I held you tight and poured comfort on your troubles and helped the tears to dry up and a smile to come back.

I am doing that now as well even if we're so far away. You have the strength of legions.

Allow the angels to help you up again. Dry your tears and give comfort to others that need it as much or more than you.

You are blessed with Godly strength. Use it to show the darkness how strong you are.

God Bless and keep you and make his face shine upon you so you can reflect it to those that need it so much.

Poppie

Nothing like the love of a father to put things back in perspective.

My friends, we have a choice. To give or give in. To give or give up. To give hope or be hopeless.

To me it's not a choice – it's a desperate need. The world needs us to shine our lights.

Together we move forward with hope.

Together we can do this.

Together, we comfort.

With Comfort & Hope,

Jen

WITH GRATITUDE

Writing a book does not bring me comfort. But there are those who kept me comforted during this process. In fact, *Showing Up* is only possible because of them:

To the Book Crew:

Skye Quinn – You are a master design genius. This book "*is* what it does" because of your vision. I am the luckiest author on the planet to be able to have you to collaborate with.

Lauren Terry – Not sure what I would have done without you. You are a powerhouse! Your layouts and infographics bring all the words to life, so people learn and remember. What a gift.

Katie Schluth – The incredible Katie: always there with calm wisdom and perspective on words and edits. Thank you doesn't cover the respect and gratitude I have for you.

Kelly Shannon – You are such a positive and passionate influence on all we do. You live and breathe this skill and help to bring it all to life in fabulous ways. You know how special you are to me.

DaMarr –For keeping us grounded and for always keeping things in perspective. You are the wind beneath my wings and the glue that holds the vision together. I love you more than you can ever know.

Eve Dreher – The master wordsmith that has allowed us to not only *name* this book, but also to *frame* it with incredible grace and depth. You are a word wizard with a remarkable heart. I am in grateful awe.

To the Comfort Crew:

My parents Dave & Betty - For always being there for me. Always. For teaching me all I need to know about human care. If everyone in the world lived like you do, there would be no need for this book.

My sisters Julie & Renata who are the most devoted sisters of all. We've never had to have a chaperone no sir. I'm there to keep my eye on her. Caring and sharing. Forever besties.

My Extended Tribe – Dick, Susie, Ian, Ralph, Cara, Doc, Hunter, Garreth, Warren, Linda, Dan, Liz, Kelsey, Caroline, Dan, Lauren, Kayla, Colin & Rosemary. Where are we without family? Love you all.

To Mary & Jill – From Cozy Marshmallows to Taco Tragedies, this book would not have happened had you not been there to help lay the foundation. As we continue to mold the vision, I am beyond grateful for your wisdom and guidance.

Bill Yetman – The sensational instructional design genius whose brain is ginormous, but his heart is even larger. Thank you doesn't come close to describing the gratitude I have for you.

Our Certified Trainers who spread comfort every day: Jeanene Hupy, Liz Riggs, Linda Marr, Julie Wall, Kim Bepko, Deb Dietrich, Steph Soza Marsh, RozLilia Salgado, Kristin Balcombe, Sandra Brown Ore, Gina Palmer, Phillip Tyler.

Our Organizational Trainers and Project Comfort Facilitators – you take comfort out every day in your own little corner of the world in beautiful ways. Thank you!

Brian, Eric, & the team at New Degree Publishing: For allowing the vision to flourish in whatever way that needs to be.

Contributors to the book: For gracing us with your beautiful words and sharing your stories: Betty Reul, Julie Wall, Laura Mayer, Daniel Mattila, Matthew Henry, Kelly Shannon, Phillip Martin, Kim & Ellie Bepko, Barb & Paige Tarpey, Bill & Adriann Nelson, Claude Silver, Mika Cross and Frits van Paasschen.

For bringing science to the skill: Dr. David DeSteno, Dr. Lynn Allen, Dr. Gabe Lomas, Dr. John Draper, Pat Breux, Jeremy Fox, Carrie Masia and Taylor Walls.

Modern Litho – The TLC you give to every book is unprecedented. Thank you!

Bryan, Ashley, Carson, Marjie, Mitchell, Morgan & Julia – So grateful for each of you and the path we are forging.

Delaine Mazich, Dunbar Okeson, Natalie Rogers, Dr. Julie Green, Carey Hitchcock, Magda Clyne, Patti Hulett, Lynne Rose, Katie Pelson & Simone Cichanowicz – my sisters forever.

John Maxwell and the JMT DNA

For believing in the mission of comfort: Colleen McFarland, Tricia Cook, Angela Allen, Deb Knupp, Andrea Mac, Amy Bontrager, Mwita, Dan Gillman, Beth Cronin & Liz Feld,

SOURCES

P. 18-19

Kix, Paul. "65,000 Teddy Bears for Newtown, and One Man to Sort the World's Grief." The Trace. December 2015. https://www.thetrace.org/2015/12/sandy-hook-shooting-donations/

Maynor, Ashley. "The Story of the Stuff." Web documentary. April 2015. http://thestoryofthestuff.com/

Williamson, Elizabeth. "A Lesson of Sandy Hook: 'Err on the Side of the Victims'." The New York Times. May 2019. https://www.nytimes.com/2019/05/25/us/politics/sandy-hook-money.html

Empathy, Sympathy, Compassion, and the Action Gap
P. 25

Data from surveys administered during Inspiring Comfort programming. 2020-2021.

Timeline of Human Care
P. 32-33

Barratt, Jane. "We are living longer than ever. But are we living better?" STAT. February 2017. https://www.statnews.com/2017/02/14/living-longer-living-better-aging/

Hawes, Catherine and Phillips, Charles D. 1986. "The Changing Structure of the Nursing Home Industry and the Impact of Ownership on Quality, Cost, and Access" in *For-Profit Enterprise in Healthcare*, edited by Bradford H. Gray. Washington, D.C.: National Academies Press, 1986.

Bethune, Sophie and Lewan, Elizabeth. "Stress About Health Insurance Costs Reported By Majority of Americans, APA Stress in America Survey Reveals." American Psychological Association. January 2018. https://www.apa.org/news/press/releases/2018/01/insurance-costs

Suris, Alina, Holliday, Ryan, and North, Carol S. 2016. "The Evolution of the Classification of Psychiatric Disorders." *Behavioral Sciences* 6, no. 1 (March): 5.

Hogg, Peter. "The top 10 medical advances in history." Proclinical. June 2021. https://www.proclinical.com/blogs/2017-11/the-top-10-medical-advances-in-history

iTalk. "A Brief History of the Home Telephone." iTalk. Accessed April 2019. https://www.italktelecom.co.uk/blog/a-brief-history-of-the-home-telephone

Polimédio, Chayenne. "Church Attendance and the Decline of Civic Spaces." Pacific Standard. November 2017. https://psmag.com/social-justice/losing-our-religion-and-its-spaces

Fischer, Molly. "What Happens When Work Becomes a Nonstop Chat Room." Intelligencer. May 2017. http://nymag.com/intelligencer/2017/05/what-has-slack-done-to-the-office.html

Riess, Jana. "Religion declining in importance for many Americans, especially for Millennials." Religion News Service. December 2018. https://religionnews.com/2018/12/10/religion-declining-in-importance-for-many-americans-especially-for-millennials/

Why We Need Comfort Now
P. 35

Centers for Disease Control and Prevention. "Drug Overdose Deaths in the U.S. Top 100,000 Annually." National Center for Health Statistics. November 2021. https://www.cdc.gov/nchs/pressroom/nchs_press_releases/2021/20211117.htm

Johns Hopkins Medicine. "Mental Health Disorder Statistics." Johns Hopkins Medicine. Accessed December 2021. https://www.hopkinsmedicine.org/health/wellness-and-prevention/mental-health-disorder-statistics

Open Minds. "The U.S. Mental Health Market: $225.1 Billion In Spending In 2019: An *OPEN MINDS* Market Intelligence Report." Open Minds. May 2020. https://openminds.com/intelligence-report/the-u-s-mental-health-market-225-1-billion-in-spending-in-2019-an-open-minds-market-intelligence-report/

National Institute of Mental Health. "Suicide." National Institute of Mental Health. Accessed December 2021. https://www.nimh.nih.gov/health/statistics/suicide

National Alliance on Mental Illness. "Anxiety Disorders." National Alliance on Mental Illness. Last reviewed December 2017. https://www.nami.org/About-Mental-Illness/Mental-Health-Conditions/Anxiety-Disorders

Harvard Graduate School of Education. "Loneliness in America: How the Pandemic Has Deepened an Epidemic of Loneliness and What We Can Do About It." Making Caring Common Project. February 2021. https://mcc.gse.harvard.edu/reports/loneliness-in-america

Numbers Behind the Need
P. 40 41

Howley, Elaine K. "What Mental Health Statistics Can Tell Us." U.S. News & World Report. June 2019. https://health.usnews.com/conditions/mental-health/articles/what-mental-health-statistics-can-tell-us

Boston University School of Public Health, Mary Christie Foundation, and Healthy Minds Network. "The Role of Faculty in Student Mental Health." Mary Christie Institute. April 2021. https://marychristieinstitute.org/wp-content/uploads/2021/04/The-Role-of-Faculty-in-Student-Mental-Health.pdf

Harvard Graduate School of Education. "Loneliness in America: How the Pandemic Has Deepened an Epidemic of Loneliness and What We Can Do About It." Making Caring Common Project. February 2021. https://mcc.gse.harvard.edu/reports/loneliness-in-america

SocialPro. "US Loneliness Statistics and Data 2021." SocialPro. Last reviewed July 2021. https://socialpronow.com/loneliness-statistics/

Centers for Disease Control and Prevention. 2020. "Mental Health, Substance Use, and Suicidal Ideation During the COVID-19 Pandemic — United States, June 24–30, 2020." *Morbidity and Mortality Weekly Report* 69, no. 32 (August): 1049-57.

Porter, Brad. "Loneliness Might Be A Bigger Health Risk Than Smoking Or Obesity." Forbes. January 2017. https://www.forbes.com/sites/quora/2017/01/18/loneliness-might-be-a-bigger-health-risk-than-smoking-or-obesity/#6d4e1cde25d1

Crist, Carolyn. "Suicide Rates Declined in 2020, But Not for All Groups, CDC Says." WebMD. November 2021. https://www.webmd.com/mental-health/news/20211103/suicide-rates-2020-cdc

Auman-Bauer, Kristie. "Research explores kinless population of older adults in the U.S." The Pennsylvania State University. October 2017. https://www.psu.edu/news/research/story/research-explores-kinless-population-older-adults-us/

Steingold, Daniel. "Survey: Most Millennials, Gen Z Adults Prefer Texting Over Talking In Person." StudyFinds. October 2017. https://www.studyfinds.org/millennials-gen-z-communicate-texting/

Jackson, Chris and Ballard, Negar. "Over Half of Americans Report Feeling Like No One Knows Them Well." Ipsos. May 2018. https://www.ipsos.com/en-us/news-polls/us-loneliness-index-report

The Dangers of Isolation
P. 45

Cabeca, Anna. "Why Do I Feel Disconnected? The Cortisol-Oxytocin Connection." Dr. Sara Gottfried MD. July 2014. https://www.saragottfriedmd.com/why-do-i-feel-disconnected-the-cortisol-oxytocin-connection/

McGonigal, Kelly. "How to make stress your friend." Filmed June 2013. TED video, 14:16. https://www.ted.com/talks/kelly_mcgonigal_how_to_make_stress_your_friend?rid=QzcBM7VMfA4j

CBS Sunday Morning. "How caring letters prevent suicide." Filmed January 2020. YouTube video, 8:28. https://www.youtube.com/watch?v=36bk3V__hZ8

It Will Take All of Us
P. 46

Data from surveys administered during Inspiring Comfort programming. 2020-2021.

The Circle of Comfort
P. 62-67

Lim, Daniel and DeSteno, David. 2016. "Suffering and Compassion: The Links Among Adverse Life Experiences, Empathy, Compassion, and Prosocial Behavior." *Emotion* 16, no. 2 (March): 175-82.

Bartlett, Monica Y. and DeSteno, David. 2006. "Gratitude and prosocial behavior: helping when it costs you." *Psychological Science* 17, no. 4 (April): 319-25.

Konrath, Sara. "The Caring Cure: Can Helping Others Help Yourself?" Psychology Today. August 2013. https://www.psychologytoday.com/us/blog/the-empathy-gap/201308/the-caring-cure-can-helping-others-help-yourself

Macro Stressors
P. 85

Miller, Mark A. and Rahe, Richard H. 1997. "Life changes scaling for the 1990s." *Journal of Psychosomatic Research* 43, no. 3 (September): 279-92.

Micro Stressors
P. 86-87

Tahmaseb-McConatha, Jasmin. "Coping with Micro-Stressors: How Do I Work My Smart TV?" Psychology Today. June 2017. https://www.psychologytoday.com/us/blog/live-long-and-prosper/201706/coping-micro-stressors-how-do-i-work-my-smart-tv

Cross, Rob, Singer, Jean, and Dillon, Karen. "Don't Let Micro-Stresses Burn You Out." Harvard Business Review. July 2020. https://hbr.org/2020/07/dont-let-micro-stresses-burn-you-out

Renner, Ben. "Stress Mess: 3 In 5 Millennials Say Life More Stressful Now Than Ever Before." StudyFinds. March 2019. https://www.studyfinds.org/survey-millennials-life-more-stressful-than-ever-before/

Ears
P. 104-109

Itzchakov, Guy and Kluger, Avraham N. "The Power of Listening in Helping People Change." Harvard Business Review. May 2018. https://hbr.org/2018/05/the-power-of-listening-in-helping-people-change

Gentry, William A., Weber, Todd J., and Sadri, Golnaz. "Empathy in the Workplace: A Tool for Effective Leadership," Center for Creative Leadership. April 2015. https://www.ccl.org/wp-content/uploads/2015/04/EmpathyInTheWorkplace.pdf

McReynolds, Marcia. "Statistics." Listening Planet. Accessed May 2019. http://www.thelisteningcards.com/statistics

Eyes
P. 110-119

Mehrabian, Albert. *Silent Messages: Implicit Communication of Emotions and Attitudes, 2nd edition*. Belmont, CA: Wadsworth Publishing Company, 1980.

American Foundation for Suicide Prevention. "Risk factors, protective factors, and warning signs." Accessed May 2019. https://afsp.org/risk-factors-protective-factors-and-warning-signs

Creating a Culture of Care
P. 162-171

De Smet, Aaron et al. "'Great Attrition' or 'Great Attraction'? The choice is yours." McKinsey Quarterly. September 2021. https://www.mckinsey.com/business-functions/people-and-organizational-performance/our-insights/great-attrition-or-great-attraction-the-choice-is-yours

Robinson, Bryan. "New EY Research Reveals The Secret Sauce To 'The Great Resignation'." Forbes. October 2021. https://www.forbes.com/sites/bryanrobinson/2021/10/16/new-ey-research-reveals-the-secret-sauce-to-the-great-resignation/?sh=207608b68068

Hotel Business. "Best Places to Work: The driving factors behind a successful hospitality culture." Hotel Business. September 2019. https://togo.hotelbusiness.com/article/best-places-to-work-the-driving-factors-behind-a-successful-hospitality-culture/

The Magic of a Dog
P. 178-179

Feldman, Steven. "For Better Mental Health, Experience the Pet Effect." Mental Health America. August 2017. http://www.mentalhealthamerica.net/blog/better-mental-health-experience-pet-effect

Maguire, Sharon. "Understanding a Dog's Senses." Dog Breed Info Center. August 2016. https://www.dogbreedinfo.com/articles/dogsenses.htm

Leotaud, Marissa. "Can Dogs Smell Our Emotions?" Cuteness. Accessed April 2019. https://www.cuteness.com/13712832/can-dogs-smell-our-emotions

VetInfo. "Dog Communication: How Dogs Talk to Humans and Each Other." VetInfo. Accessed April 2019. https://www.vetinfo.com/dog-communication.html

Shojai, Amy. "Understanding Dog Talk." The Spruce Pets. Last updated October 2021. https://www.thesprucepets.com/dog-language-understanding-dog-talk-2804565

Keeps, David A. "The Science Behind How Dogs Make Us Happier, Healthier, and Fitter." Men's Journal. Accessed April 2019. https://www.mensjournal.com/health-fitness/the-science-behind-how-dogs-make-us-happier-healthier-and-fitter-w431916/

PHOTO CREDITS
(agency is iStockphoto except where indicated otherwise)

COVER
wundervisuals/ Getty Images

TYPOGRAPHY
Clelsea Kardokus

BACK FLAP
Peter Friedman, courtesy of TIME

CONTENTS
Lara Belova

THE CASE FOR COMFORT
16-17 Layla Bird, 22-23 Adobe Stock, 29 clu, 32-33 Library of Congress, (3) Adobe Stock (17), 34 Alex Vucha Photography, 36-39 photos courtesy of subjects, 42 Adobe Stock

THE PROCESS
48-49 Alex Vucha Photography, 50-51 VLG, 54-61 Antonio Guillem, martin-dm, Courtney Hale, Adobe Stock, Emir Memedovski, 63 Jen Marr, 71 Kali9, 72-73 Adam Kaz, 76-77 Juanmonino, 78 Adobe Stock 79 Ekely22, 82-83 iiievgeniy, 89 Kim Bepko

SHOWING UP
90-91 skynesher, 92-93 EllenaZ, 98-99 Solaris Images, 102-103 bloodstone, 104-105 Pixel Fusion 3D, 110-111 XiXinXing, 114-115 shutterstock, 120-121 Denia Fernandez, 126-127 fizkes, 128-129 Enes Evren, 130-131 Chaay Tee, 132-133 No-System Images, 135 Jen Marr, 136-137 PeopleImages, 138-141 mikkelwilliam, pollyana Ventura 142 Francesco Corticchia, 144-145 PKpix, 146-147 Monkey Business Images, 148 Katarzyna Bialasiewicz, 149 LightFieldStudios, 150-151 sudok1, 152 Aleksandar Nakic, 153 PeopleImages, 154 SDI Productions, 155 Vasyl Dolmatov, 156-157 Antonio Guillem 158-158 fotoglee

CULTURE OF CARE
162-163 Adobe Stock 164-171 Adobe Stock, *Hotel Business* September 2019 174-175 Adobe Stock

WHO SHOWS UP BEST
178-179 Ultra Marin Foto, 180-181 Rasulovs, 182 Christin Lola, 183 George Peters, 184 SeventyFour, fcscafeine, 185 blanscape, 186 Team Jackson, 187 Adam Kaz, 188 Casarsa Guru, 189 PeopleImages, 190-191 Maksim Kamyshanskii, 192 supersizer, 193 sonjaarose, 194-195 Chalabala, 196 Erik Lam, 197 Chesire Cat, 198 dageldog, 199 Hannah Wade

NOTES

WHO IS INSPIRING COMFORT?

Inspiring Comfort is a social good company founded on the belief that today's socially disconnected and hurting world demands we do a better job of caring for one another.

Our evidence-based Comfort Skills Programming is here to close the gap by creating cultures of comfort in 4 steps:

Assess: We evaluate your current care culture through surveys and individual assessments.

Inform: We bring awareness to the need for comfort through in-person and virtual presentations.

Equip: We provide program participants with the tools to break through the Awkward Zone and connect with those around them.

Cultivate: We certify your staff as facilitators of our programs to grow and maintain a culture of comfort.

WORK WITH US

HOW WE TRAIN

We offer these three levels of training. We can also create custom training for your group.

FUNDAMENTALS

INCLUDES

Keynote
Executive Briefing

Assessments/Surveys

The Awkward Zone Workshop

CORE

INCLUDES
FUNDAMENTALS
+

Team Connections Workshop

Lead With Heart Workshop

Showing Up Books for Participants

CERTIFICATIONS

INCLUDES
CORE
+

Train the Trainer Programs

Facilitation Training

Quarterly Coaching Calls

Combined Group & Online Training

WHO WE TRAIN

Workplaces / Organizations / Leaders / Colleges & Universities / Youth

PROJECT COMFORT

Project Comfort is a youth character development program with eight valuable lessons. We certify your staff to facilitate the program.

BOOK A PROGRAM:

WEBSITE:
INSPIRINGCOMFORT.COM/PROGRAMS

EMAIL:
INFO@INSPIRINGCOMFORT.COM

JOIN OUR COMMUNITY:

FACEBOOK: *INSPIRING COMFORT*

LINKEDIN: *INSPIRING COMFORT*
LINKEDIN: *JEN MARR*

INSTAGRAM: *@INSPIRINGCOMFORT*

QUOTES TO REMEMBER

"The most important quality in a mentor, teacher, or coach is not how much they know. It's how much they care"
–ADAM GRANT

"Attention is the rarest and purest form of generosity."
—SIMONE WEIL

"Watch carefully, the magic that occurs, when you give a person just enough comfort, to be themselves."
–ATTICUS

"AFTER MORE THAN FORTY YEARS OF BEING A COUNSELOR, I'M CONVINCED THAT AS MANY AS ONE-THIRD TO ONE-HALF OF ALL THE PEOPLE I'VE SEEN WOULDN'T HAVE NEEDED TO SEE ME IF THEY'D HAD A KNOWLEDGEABLE FRIEND."
–H. NORMAN WRIGHT

"Although the world is full of suffering, it is full also of the overcoming of it."
–HELEN KELLER

"It is in the shelter of each other that the people live."
–IRISH PROVERB

"If you want to make someone feel cared for, notice them. Talk to them. Show them that they aren't living unnoticed. Be nice. Be a decent human being. Allow yourself to make connections because it's the connections we make, that decide the lives we lead."
—P. HUDSON